Under the Official Secrets Act 1989, Chapter 6,

subsection 1, a person who is or has been

a member of the security and intelligence

services is guilty of an offence if without

lawful authority he

discloses any information, document or other article

relating to security or intelligence which is or has been

in his possession by virtue of his position as a member

of any of those services or in the course of his work

while the notification ... was in force, is ...

that a disclosure of this kind is ... by the provisions of this Act

ALEX RIDER MISSION FILES

ANTHONY HOROWITZ

Writer and researcher: Emil Fortune

Technical illustrator: John Lawson

Rostrum photography: John Peacock

WALKER BOOKS
AND SUBSIDIARIES

LONDON · BOSTON · SYDNEY · AUCKLAND

CONTENTS

INTRODUCTION

Welcome to the complete Alex Rider dossier, a behind-the-scenes look at the world of the seven books in the series. In here you'll find new information about the characters, locations and events of the novels as well as a short story – "Christmas at Gunpoint" – which describes an incident in the early life of Alex and which I originally wrote for a national newspaper. It's here in book form for the first time.

It's been nearly ten years since I wrote the first sentence of *Stormbreaker*, the first Alex Rider novel – "When the doorbell rings at three in the morning, it's never good news" – and, in doing so, changed my life. Since then, more than ten million copies have been sold in twenty-five countries and I have versions on my shelves that baffle even me. I mean, could you guess which Alex title and which language is represented by the following: *Pelikuningas*, *Insel des Schreckens*, *Topphemligt*, *Ostrov Kostlivců*, *Tarandon*, *Simsekkiran*? (Answers at the end of this introduction.)

From the very start, I made two decisions about the Alex Rider books.

First of all, they wouldn't be "children's" books. I wanted to write tough, relatively serious stories that I thought of as "adult books for kids". They would take place in the MI6 of the modern world: untrustworthy, cold, manipulative ... the sort of organization nobody would want to work for. Alex would be a real teenager. He would find himself trapped in this world against his will and he wouldn't enjoy it. He would get hurt. And – if he had to – he would kill.

Almost at once I got into trouble. Although my publishers supported the idea of Alex Rider (and gave the first edition of *Stormbreaker* a perfect adult cover – fluorescent green with a streak of lightning slicing down the middle) they were immediately concerned about levels of violence. They insisted that Alex should never have a gun.

It's easy to see why. Guns and kids don't go well together. You only have to look at the horror stories coming out of America – high school shootings, etc – to understand why they were so nervous. Anyway, when I saw this was one argument I was never going to win, I decided to make a virtue out of necessity. Alex wants a gun but never gets one. All his gadgets are non-lethal. And although he does fire guns later in the series (in *Scorpia* he even takes a shot at Mrs Jones) he never actually hits anyone.

The second decision I made was that these books would be as realistic as possible. I'm often asked why I spend so much time describing machinery and weapons. The Yamaha Mountain Max snowmobiles with their 700 cc triple-cylinder engines in *Point Blanc*, for example. Or the FP9 single-action pistols in *Ark Angel*. The reason is simple. When I'm writing the big, set-piece action sequences that crop up in each Alex book, I want them to be completely believable. And it seems to me that the more technical detail I throw in (without getting boring), the more likely it is that the reader will accept Alex's more fantastic adventures.

It's all the research that makes a book like this possible. Basically, everything you read in an Alex Rider story is based on fact – from the workings of a car crusher (*Stormbreaker*) to how a tsunami is created (*Snakehead*). I try to visit every location so I can describe it accurately. I actually watched a car crusher, for example. I climbed and operated a crane for *Point Blanc*. I was invited underneath the famous tennis courts at Wimbledon for *Skeleton Key* and went to a bull fight (ugh!) for *Eagle Strike*.

Sometimes I move things around. In *Eagle Strike*, Damian Cray's home in Bath with its bizarre garden full of miniature buildings does exist, but not in England. It's actually a villa that I stumbled upon when I was on holiday in Montegiove in Italy. Whenever I travel, I take a notebook with me, jotting down ideas and locations for a future book. The Church of Forgotten Saints in *Scorpia* was inspired by the Brompton Oratory in west London. And even Alex's school, Brookland, is based on a school with the same name that I used to visit. But it's in Finchley, not Chelsea.

Most of the locations, however, are 100 per cent accurate. I often visit cities to work out a chase step by step – Venice for *Scorpia* and Amsterdam for *Eagle Strike*, for example. I stood on the balcony at Ravello, planning Alex's base jump in *Scorpia* (although I had to imagine the factory below) – and if you want to, you can even have lunch at the Hotel Sirenuse in Positano, where he meets Mrs Rothman. I couldn't have written the

shoot-out at the end of *Snakehead* without spending a day on an oil rig near Aberdeen. Photographs will only show you so much: you actually have to go there to get a sense of the mud, the oil, the grease – the sheer hardness of the place.

There have only been two locations that I've been unable to visit, for obvious reasons. I couldn't go into outer space (*Ark Angel*) but I talked at length to Dr Michael Foale, who had. And the White House wouldn't let me visit Air Force One (*Eagle Strike*). I had to cheat by watching films and TV programmes that had reconstructed the aircraft – *The West Wing* is said to be the most accurate.

And while we're on the subject of reality, you might like to know that all the Alex books have been inspired by true stories. It often happens that my first inspiration comes from an article I've noticed in the newspapers. The cloning of a sheep was the starting point of *Point Blanc*. The sinking of a Russian nuclear submarine in the Barents Sea (12 August 2000) set me off on the story that became *Skeleton Key*. Richard Branson's plan to build a hotel in outer space inspired *Ark Angel*. *Snakehead* began with the pop singer, Bob Geldoff (who actually appears in the book … I call him Rob Goldman). I hope this is what sets Alex's adventures apart from films like *Agent Cody Banks* and *Spy Kids*. As fantastic as some of the stories may sometimes seem, at heart he belongs to the real world.

For me, the most important thing to get right is the gadgets. I have two rules. They have to be non-lethal. But more importantly, they have to be credible. I really hated the James Bond films that had completely impossible gadgets – X-ray spectacles, matchbox-sized oxygen tanks or, worst of all, the invisible car in *Die Another Day*. How can you believe a story when it's got something that's obviously absurd in the middle? To give you an idea of how closely we stick to the truth, a library in the north of England actually banned *Alex Rider: The Gadgets* because they believed kids might use it to create their own lethal weapons! And when I wrote *Ark Angel*, the publishers made me put a warning in the back in case any of my readers broke their necks trying funambulism ... or tightrope-walking.

Having mentioned James Bond, I ought to acknowledge the debt that I owe to the films and also to the wonderful books written by Ian Fleming. As I've often said, Alex Rider was originally inspired by my feeling that James Bond was getting too old. Did you know that when Roger Moore played Bond for the last time he was fifty-eight? That's old enough to be Alex's grandfather! One day I thought to myself, wouldn't it be great if Bond were a teenager again? And in that moment Alex Rider was born.

However, I have worked hard to make Alex as different from Bond as possible. There's no point stealing someone else's ideas, so I spend a lot of time thinking up action sequences that Bond hasn't done – being chased down a ski slope on a converted ironing board, for example. Or becoming the central character in a live-action and lethal computer game. Or using a heart machine, a medicine ball and an MRI scanner in a hospital to knock out your enemies. Originally I wasn't even going to have gadgets in the books – I thought it would be too close to the films. I only added them in the second draft of *Stormbreaker* because whenever I visited schools, people were always disappointed that there weren't any.

Anyway, I hope you enjoying delving into Alex's world: the codes, the spycraft, the blueprints and the various shadowy characters. By the way, did you know that one of the villains in one of the books didn't really die? Or that Smithers has a big secret which I don't plan to reveal until the last book? And whatever happened to Alex's clone...?

One day, perhaps, you'll find out.

Anthony Horowitz
September 2008

PS The book titles are: *Eagle Strike* in Finnish, *Skeleton Key* in German, *Point Blanc* in Dutch, *Skeleton Key* in Czech, *Stormbreaker* in Welsh and *Stormbreaker* in Turkish!

A VERY SPECIAL OPERATION

MI6 and Alex Rider

ALEX RIDER: TEENAGE SPY

Alex Rider was catapulted from schoolboy to superspy following the death of his uncle. The nature of Alex's work for MI6 was a closely guarded secret, but limited data was eventually released to the Australian secret service upon request.

TOP SECRET:

REPORT SUBJECT: ALEX RIDER

Mr Brooke: here's everything we have on the Rider boy. MI6 in the UK have been very cagey about releasing information – I suspect because he's a high-value operative. M.D.

PHYSICAL DESCRIPTION/ATTRIBUTES

Age: 14

D.O.B.: 13 February 1987

Height: 5'4"/162.6 cm *Still short for his age, but t[...] to his operational value.*

Weight: 120 lb/54.4 kg

Hair colour: Fair

Eyes: Brown

Physical condition: Excellent *But may have been compromised by recent injuries?*

Skills: Black belt in karate

Rock-climbing and mountaineering (IML part 1)

Diving (PADI Advanced Open Water/Junior Rescue Diver)

Fluent in French and Spanish; proficient in German

Physical training: British SAS 426-1 (passed)

Weapons training: None *From what we've heard, this guy's a lethal weapon already.*

PSYCHOLOGICAL PROFILE

AR was recruited by MI6 Special Operations in March of this year, aged fourteen. His father was John Rider – alias Hunter – who was killed in action. His mother died at the same time and he was brought up by his uncle, Ian Rider, also an active agent with MI6 before his death earlier this year. It seems certain that the boy was physically and mentally prepared for intelligence work from the earliest age.

Despite his obvious aptitude for it, AR has shown little enthusiasm for espionage. Like most teenagers, he is not a patriot and has no interest in politics. MI6 (SO) found it necessary to coerce him to work for them on at least two occasions.

Popular at school – when he is there. Recent progress has been slow, with negative feedback from many of his teachers. However, it must be remembered that AR has been absent from class for much of the past eight months; a report from his summer tutor (Charlie Grey) shows good mental ability.

Hobbies include football (Chelsea supporter), tennis, music and cinema. AR also competes in the junior league at his local pool and snooker club and represented his class in the pole vault at a recent school sports day. Evident interest in girls – see separate file on Sabina Pleasure and report by CIA operative Tamara Knight. Lives with American housekeeper, Jack Starbright (note: despite first name, Jack is female).

No ambitions to follow his father and uncle into intelligence.

PAST ASSIGNMENTS – ACTIVE SERVICE

The British secret service refuses to admit that it has ever employed a juvenile, and so it has been difficult to draw together any concrete evidence of AR's record as an agent in the field. We believe, however, that he has worked for them on at least four occasions. He has also been seconded to the USA, where he has been employed by the CIA with equal success at least twice.

Although it has so far proved impossible to confirm details, it would appear that in the space of one year AR has been involved in at least six major assignments, succeeding against impossible odds.

CURRENT STATUS: Available

Last year the FBI attempted to recruit a teenage agent to combat drug syndicates operating out of Miami. The boy was killed almost immediately. The experiment has not been repeated.

THE PUBLIC FACE OF MI6

The Secret Intelligence Service (SIS), more commonly known as MI6, is home to foreign intelligence operations serving to protect the UK's national security.

The headquarters of MI6, located in Vauxhall, London, is a landmark synonymous with covert activity, housing the nerve centre of British Foreign Intelligence. From within its bulletproof walls it manages a small army of spies, analysts and technical experts all around the world.

Built like a garrison, MI6 uses stringent security measures that range from CCTV to triple-glazed windows to prevent electronic eavesdropping and the jamming of communication networks. Much of the building's distinctive structure (earning it the nickname "Legoland") exists below ground to guard against terrorist attack.

Applicants to the SIS undergo a rigorous vetting process that leaves no aspect of their past unchecked. This can take several months to complete, and an entrant's success is dependent on him or her posing absolutely no threat to the UK's national security.

Newly recruited agents are immediately placed on the Intelligence Officers' New Entry Course (IONEC), which lasts

MI6 headquarters:
MI6's London base is a large and conspicuous building on the south side of the River Thames.

TOP SECRET

MI6 NEW AGENT PAMPHLET

This booklet, disguised as a regional bus timetable, is given to all MI6 agents at the start of the induction process. It introduces key terms which they will need to become familiar with in their work.

... for six months and is designed to prepare them for their unique career in the secret service. Here they will acquire skills that include essential techniques in espionage, known as tradecraft.

Over the duration of the course agents are subjected to a variety of discreet tasks. Assignments can be anything from obtaining the name, address and passport number of a complete stranger to breaking into and entering the house of a member of the public to plant a fake bugging device.

Tradecraft tests often pit agents against teams from other services such as MI5 (the Security Service) or the Army Intelligence Corps. The aim of these exercises is for each team to complete their mission without the knowledge of the other. An example might be to complete a successful brush pass, i.e. the transmission of a document or piece of information between agents, in a crowded space, without the transmitter being identified.

The agent will eventually be sent overseas for their final trial, a covert mission to be carried out under the nose of a foreign police force or security system. If the agent is caught, he or she is unlikely to be considered for fieldwork in the future.

Secret agents must not discuss details of their jobs with colleagues and are forbidden to reveal to friends or family what they do for a living. The only member of the SIS whose name and face is known to the public is, in fact, the chief.

THE ROYAL & GENERAL BANK

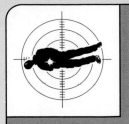

MI6's Special Operations department is based at the Royal & General Bank in Liverpool Street. The majority of the building is off-limits to the public but is revealed in this schematic.

While most Londoners are familiar with the conspicuous building that is MI6's headquarters at Vauxhall Cross, few are aware of the location of its most secret department: Special Operations. This is housed in an entirely different part of London in the Royal & General Bank, an unexceptional seventeen-storey building near Liverpool Street Station.

17th floor: The mainframe computer is housed on the top floor in a secure "ops room", where TEMPEST shielding safeguards against the laser and radio-frequency flooding techniques often employed by the enemy to infiltrate British intelligence. Reporting to the head of Special Operations, highly skilled analysts and officers work night and day monitoring the global activities of their agents. A concealed satellite array, positioned on the roof, enables Special Ops to link with MI6 HQ and exchange information.

16th–15th floors: Highly ranked officers, field agents, intelligence experts and managers will often be required to work around the clock, sleeping and eating on the job. The 15th floor offers agents good rest facilities: bunk beds are situated in rooms secured by magnetic locks, and each officer is issued a safe with a unique personal code in which to place his or her belongings – including top-secret files. In the event of tampering, these storage units are designed to collapse internally, preventing all access.

13th floor: The head of Research and Development (R&D) works from his 13th-floor office, which has been modified with a variety of experimental devices, including concealed video screens, a weapons detector built into his desk lamp and an electrical device for vaporizing secret documents.

17

16

15

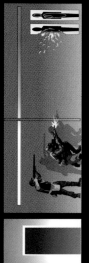

11

10

G

BUREAU DE CHANGE

B

11th–10th floors: Here R&D tests and develops all its inventions, in a series of fully equipped laboratories containing everything from mass spectrometers to crash-test dummies. A team of sixteen scientists works here full time, supplemented by special consultants with expertise in toxicology, explosives, cryptography, firearms and electronics. The area is soundproofed and insulated from the rest of the building by Class III biological containment systems.

Ground floor: On street level the building appears and functions just like any high street bank and is open to the public; some – but not all – of the bank staff are aware of the nature of the rest of the building. A lift to the upper levels conceals a CS 5000 weapons detector as well as X-ray scanners for bombs and chemical, biological and radiological weapons and unauthorized telecommunications equipment.

Basements: The subterranean part of Special Operations is accessed by lifts on the 5th floor, and is again restricted to MI6 personnel. A soundproof shooting range enables strobe gun target practice, while a fully equipped gym allows operatives to stay in shape. Below this is an interrogation room equipped with a two-way mirror and holding cells. In addition, military tanks and specially modified vehicles are housed in secure basement garages.

SPECIAL OPERATIONS

The chief executive of Special Operations, Alan Blunt, heads up a highly skilled team assisted by his deputy, Mrs Jones.

Issued by the ADMIN DEPT – Document No. ADM

STRUCTURE OF MI6 SPECIAL OPERATIONS

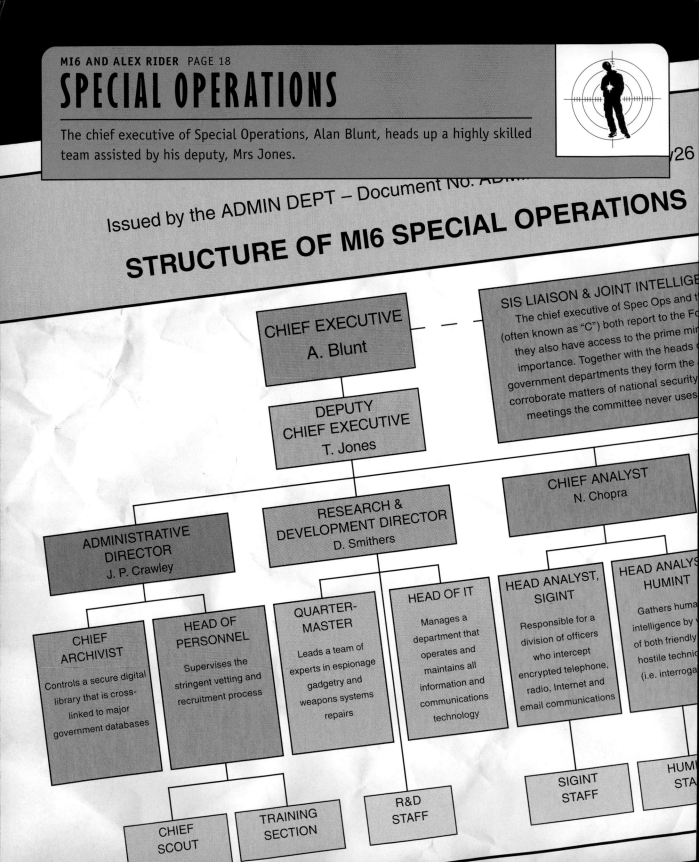

CHIEF EXECUTIVE
A. Blunt

DEPUTY CHIEF EXECUTIVE
T. Jones

SIS LIAISON & JOINT INTELLIGE

The chief executive of Spec Ops and t
(often known as "C") both report to the Fo
they also have access to the prime min
importance. Together with the heads
government departments they form the
corroborate matters of national security
meetings the committee never uses

CHIEF ANALYST
N. Chopra

ADMINISTRATIVE DIRECTOR
J. P. Crawley

RESEARCH & DEVELOPMENT DIRECTOR
D. Smithers

CHIEF ARCHIVIST

Controls a secure digital library that is cross-linked to major government databases

HEAD OF PERSONNEL

Supervises the stringent vetting and recruitment process

QUARTER-MASTER

Leads a team of experts in espionage gadgetry and weapons systems repairs

HEAD OF IT

Manages a department that operates and maintains all information and communications technology

HEAD ANALYST, SIGINT

Responsible for a division of officers who intercept encrypted telephone, radio, Internet and email communications

HEAD ANALYS HUMINT

Gathers huma intelligence by of both friendly hostile technic (i.e. interroga

CHIEF SCOUT

TRAINING SECTION

R&D STAFF

SIGINT STAFF

HUM STA

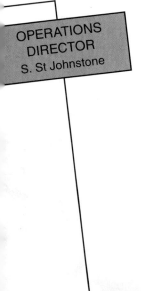

COMMITTEE

...all chief of MI6
...secretary, although
...r matters of high
...GCHQ and other
...ch meets weekly to
...lieved that for these
...ne location twice.

OPERATIONS DIRECTOR
S. St Johnstone

OPERATIONAL STAFF

Issued by SIS/SPEC-OPS/ADMIN – Ref. SCA36 5.2.2001

CHIEF EXECUTIVE [CE/SPEC-OPS]: Alan Blunt is in overall charge of the department, and reports directly to the Joint Intelligence Committee and the head of SIS. He is empowered to authorize covert missions overseas and (uniquely for an MI6 department) on home soil. SPEC-OPS is a "dark" department; if asked, the service will deny that it exists.

DEPUTY CHIEF EXECUTIVE [DCE/SPEC-OPS]: Day-to-day management of Special Operations is the job of Mrs T. Jones. All division heads (Admin, R&D, Analysis and Ops) report to her. The primary responsibility of Mrs Jones is to ensure the smooth running of all current assignments and to keep Alan Blunt briefed at all times.

ADMIN DIRECTOR [AD/SPEC-OPS]: John Crawley is responsible for all personnel, buildings and assets belonging to the department. Reporting to him are the head of personnel and the chief archivist. Scouting for and training new agents is also part of Crawley's role.

R&D DIRECTOR [RD/SPEC-OPS]: Derek Smithers is in charge of the department's scientific and technical staff. Smithers has a team of experts stationed at various laboratories around the world, dedicated to producing espionage equipment and covert weapons for SPEC-OPS agents.

CHIEF ANALYST [CA/SPEC-OPS]: Neel Chopra collects and analyses all information gathered by agents in the field. Analysis is split into Signals Intelligence (SIGINT) and Human Intelligence (HUMINT).

OPERATIONS DIRECTOR [OD/SPEC-OPS]: Operations staff are the agents who directly participate in secret missions on behalf of the department – either in the field or in support of those who are. Simon St Johnstone monitors the progress of mission teams, ensuring they have all the resources necessary to complete their assignments or to evade counter-intelligence.

CHIEF ARCHIVIST [CAV/SPEC-OPS]: The digital library held by the Special Operations department is an essential resource for those out in the field. In addition...
vital records, it...

RECRUITMENT

Documentation from Ian Rider's recruitment to MI6 shows the importance of absolute confidentiality and acknowledges the inherent dangers of the job.

From: Personnel
To: Administration

Ian Rider's application has been successful -- please advise him of the following:

(1) New cover to be effective immediately; he must familiarize himself with the materials contained in this dossier. He will be based at our Liverpool Street branch and has been headhunted by the Royal & General Bank, who will employ him as Overseas Finance Manager.

(2) The Department does not officially exist. He must maintain operational security at all times -- even when dealing with government employees, should they have a lower security clearance rating. If his cover is blown, the Department will disavow any knowledge of his actions.

The next batch of training starts next Wednesday. Check with Sergeant Angleton at Larkhill that there are still places -- Rider will need to do N544 (close-quarter combat). Once you get the green light, arrange schedules, tickets etc.

Remind Rider that to family and friends he will be enjoying three weeks of conferences at the School of Fiscal Policy in Frankfurt.

Dear Officer,

SENT ON BEHALF OF MI6

Enclosed is a copy of the Official Secrets Act (1920). Please read through the document carefully and be reminded that you are covered by all sections within. Failure to adhere to the terms will result in immediate dismissal, with the potential for legal action to be taken against you.

The below statement must be signed accordingly and returned with your other documents.

✂--

I have read and understood the terms and conditions set out in the Official Secrets Act (1920) and agree to be bound by them.

Signed: ....

Dated: ....

ADDITIONAL LIFE INSURANCE INFORMATION:

We hope that the following information will never be required during your service, but in the event of your death, a named beneficiary will be entitled to receive your accumulated income as well as any further compensation due.

Please give details of the named beneficiary/beneficiaries to be contacted and state the percentage of income you would like them to receive. You may name more than one beneficiary.

Name	% to be paid
1. ~~John Rider~~	~~100%~~
2. Alex Rider	100%
3.	

Signed: I Rider   Date: 31 March 1988

It is essential that you fill out this form and return it immediately. The policy will be effective from the first day of your employment.

OFFICER'S KEY CARD

Instructions for use: please destroy once these have been read and understood

Location: Royal & General Bank, Liverpool Street
Access: Entrance via street level office

Location: MI6 headquarters, Vauxhall Cross
Access: Entrance via basement office located in underground tunnel (marked on enclosed map)

DO NOT LOSE THIS CARD

Special Operations is a covert division; you must not be seen entering MI6

WARNING!
SEE SECTION 4.2 OF
SECURITY POLICY

REMOVE STICKER
TO ACTIVATE
IDENTITY CODE

SAS TRAINING

SAS counter-terrorism training of the type undertaken by Alex Rider involves the use of an imitation embassy. Recruits must make their way through it without setting off alarms or booby traps.

Special Operations field operatives are taught various forms of self-defence, including hand-to-hand combat and pistol and rifle shooting. Much of this instruction is supervised by the Special Air Services, or SAS, the world's most celebrated elite special forces group. SAS training includes exercises at the so-called Killing House, a building used to teach infiltration, close-quarter combat and hostage rescue. A typical exercise might involve a squad making its way through the building, disabling both the security systems and any "guards" stationed there to stop them.

1 **Pressure pads:** Sensors activated by weight.

2 **Laser beams:** Rays of invisible laser light that are shone across a room onto a reflector at the other side. The reflector bounces the beams back to the sensor, where they are detected by a photoelectric cell. If anything comes between the emitter and the reflector, the beams are broken and the alarm is sounded.

3 **Motion detector:** A microwave radar sensor designed to detect moving targets and trigger a .50 calibre machine gun concealed behind a screen. The sensor measures the wave-length of reflected waves and notes any changes.

4 **Tripwire:** A simple but effective booby trap made up of a single thread of mono-filament fishing line stretched across a room at ankle height. Stepping on or tripping over the wire would activate the contact trigger of a flash-bang grenade, designed to stun everybody in the room.

5 **Interior walls:** Movable partitions that allow SAS instructors to remodel the inside of the house at will. No two missions are alike.

6 **Bullet troughs:** Floor-level troughs to collect spent shells. Many of the Killing House missions involve firing live ammunition; the walls are rubberized to absorb bullet impact and prevent ricochets.

7 **CCTV:** A network of closed-circuit TV cameras monitoring all exercises throughout the house. SAS trainees who fail too many exercises risk being "binned" – i.e. returned to their regular army unit with no chance of reapplying.

COMPUTER VIRUS

Herod Sayle and the Stormbreaker

STORMBREAKER: THE BEGINNING

MI6 had had their eye on Lebanese businessman Herod Sayle for many years.

MEMO

From: John Crawley, Section 9

To: Alan Blunt (Chief executive)

Not for general circulation. Briefing document 514/445

Subject: Herod Sayle and the Stormbreaker

This department has long had suspicions regarding Herod Sayle and his much publicized gift of a Stormbreaker computer to every school in the UK. His activities in China and Russia (see files S/CH/232--235) may have fitted in with his worldwide business plan, but a possible connection with the international assassin Yassen Gregorovich could not be ignored.

Following our initial briefing, a field agent -- Ian Rider -- was sent to Sayle's manufacturing plant in Port Tallon, Cornwall. He spent three weeks there working undercover as a security guard and filed several reports in which he confirmed that everything seemed above board. However, in a subsequent message he alerted us to a possible Code One security alert. Following normal procedure, he planned his immediate return to London.

We deeply regret the loss of this highly skilled operative. Ian Rider was ambushed near Bodmin and killed by automatic gunfire. However, we must point out that his sudden death only confirms our original suspicions. It is evident that Herod Sayle is not what he seems.

This is a view shared by other divisions within MI6 Special Operations but not, unfortunately, by the government. It should be remembered that the prime minister was at school with Sayle and may have pleasant memories of that time. More to the point, with education at the centre of his party manifesto it will take more than the death of one agent to convince him that these computers should not be allowed into schools.

We believe it is now critical to place a second agent inside Port Tallon to re-examine the processing plant and follow up on any leads that may have been left by Ian Rider. This must be effected before 1 April, when the Stormbreaker computers are due to be launched at the Science Museum in west London. It will not, however, be easy. Sayle will be expecting us to do precisely this, and any new personnel will come under the closest scrutiny. We need to find someone who can slip under his radar.

We have several female agents: there are often vacancies in the kitchens and housekeeping departments at Port Tallon; if there are none currently available, it would be fairly simple to create one. But would this be good enough? Would a cook or a cleaner have access to the production areas, many of which are subterranean and under guard?

The attention of this department has been drawn to one small possibility. In what is clearly intended to be a public relations stunt, Sayle has been running a competition in the computer magazine "Disk Drive World". The winner is being offered a free tour of the facility as well as a chance to meet Herod Sayle. This might be our way in. The only problem is that the competition winner has already been announced. His name is Felix Lester and he is fourteen years old.

It might be worth speaking to Derek Smithers to ascertain whether it would be possible to disguise one of our agents as a fourteen-year-old boy. With modern prosthetics, the right clothes and hairstyle etc...

In the meantime, we are looking for alternative ways in -- but time is now running out. Ian Rider died trying to tell us something; it is imperative we find out what he discovered and why it cost him his life.

IAN RIDER HAS
A NEPHEW.

AB.

View of Trevose Head © Richard ROWSE (1996)

Published by Trevithick & Co., Padstow. No unauthorized reproduction.

Dear Alex
Its sunny down in Cornwall
but I'm not getting much of a
tan - stuck in lectures about
"New Approaches to European
Banking." Wish you were here?
We should come back for some
surfing though, you'd love it.
Back Sunday - see you then.
Ian xx

Alex Rider
140 Cheyne Wal
Chelsea
LONDON

SAYLE ENTERPRISES

Sayle's Stormbreaker project promised to break new ground.

THE STORM IS ABOUT
TO BREAK

THE STORM IS ABOUT TO BREAK

The Sayle Enterprises S13 Stormbreaker is on the cutting edge of computer science. Powered by the lightning-fast new Round Processor™, it leaves the competition thunderstruck. In tests, the Stormbreaker performed more than twice as well as the market leaders.

The Stormbreaker contains 1 GB of on-board MRAM, the most advanced memory available, enabling it to operate with maximum efficiency and speed. No more waiting around for your PC to warm up in the morning! And because of its compatibility with traditional Windows and Macintosh programs, the Stormbreaker offers unrivalled versatility: you will be surprised how familiar the future can feel.

The designers have combined this revolutionary new technology with award-winning design, too – the versatile keyboard layout offers an unsurpassable ergonomic experience for any user, and the stylish digital-ink screen displays with sharp resolution within seconds of powering up.

We're so confident the Stormbreaker will change your life that Say Enterprises will be donating one to every secondary school in the country, loaded with educational software that will exceed all you students' expectations. Learning is about to become fun again! child in Britain is going to catch the Stormbreaker bug – are yo

FLOATING-POINT MATHS

INSOLON G660 DUAL CORE

SOUTHWESTER S3 PRO SERIES

SEAGAL SYSTEMS ACCELL 4400

0   200   400   600

MOPS/S

INTEGER MATHS

INSOLON G660 DUAL COR

SOUTHWESTER S3 PRO SERIES

SEAGAL SYSTEMS ACCELL

0   100   200

MOPS/S

A PERSONAL MESSAGE FROM HEROD SAYLE

Looking back on my schooldays in England, I can see clearly that they made me the man I am today. I'll never forget the way I was treated by my classmates; they taught me the true meaning of British tolerance, honesty and fair play. These values have served me well over the years, and I am proud that, thanks to them, I have made a great success of Sayle Enterprises.

The Stormbreaker computer is the crowning triumph of my career, and it seems fitting that I should use it to repay the British people – from my old classmate the Prime Minister, to the millions of children all over the land – on behalf of the young Herod Sayle. To that end, I am donating computers to every single school in the country. I want to reach out to every child, without exception.

I am very much looking forward to the grand launch ceremony at the Science Museum, when the Prime Minister himself will throw the switch that activates the Stormbreakers. In a very real sense, he will be finishing something he started over forty years ago, when I first came to these shores, looking for a friend.

Herod

PORT TALLON INDUSTRIAL COMPLEX

Dark secrets were concealed beneath Sayle's manufacturing complex in Cornwall.

Sayle Enterprises was situated near Port Tallon, in Cornwall. As the base for his computer hardware business, Sayle had the state-of-the-art facility built from the most modern materials available.

The land had previously been the property of Sir Rupert Dozmary, whose family had owned some of the richest tin mines in England. Although it was thought that Sir Rupert blew his own brains out in 1991, following the collapse of the tin market, a subsequent autopsy revealed two bullet holes and it now seems likely that foul play was involved. The unfortunate baronet had refused to sell his ancestral home and its grounds to Sayle; his widow later accepted a reduced offer and retired to the British Virgin Islands.

Sayle's primary concern was for privacy. He fenced off five square kilometres of his new property and had it patrolled night and day by guards armed with semi-automatic machine guns. Other security measures included razor wire and surveillance cameras, and the main gate and cargo plane runway – the only official ways in or out of the complex – were used solely by employees. Unbeknown to Sayle, there was also a third entrance: a partially flooded mine shaft leading from outside the fence to the basement of the factory building (D).

Opposite the airstrip and cargo warehouse was the main factory complex, which consisted of four buildings linked by raised walkways. Building A housed the administration offices and also provided recreational facilities for the staff, with a canteen, gym and even an IMAX cinema. The Stormbreaker's operating system and applications were written and designed in Building B, with Building C used for the testing and assessment of the computer hardware. Building D was the factory. The computers were manufactured in its lower-security areas; underground, in a top-secret basement, was the assembly line installing a deadly surprise in each unit: the R5 virus delivery system.

Sayle himself lived in a sprawling mock-Victorian mansion at the end of the main drive. The fifty-bedroom house was filled with Sayle's extensive art collection and the trophies of his many big-game hunts. His most impressive souvenir was kept by the businessman as a pet – a deadly Portuguese man-of-war jellyfish that lived in a vast aquarium in Sayle's private office.

THE STORMBREAKER COMPUTER

The Stormbreaker itself was both a marvel of technology and a tool of terror.

ROUND PROCESSOR HOUSING

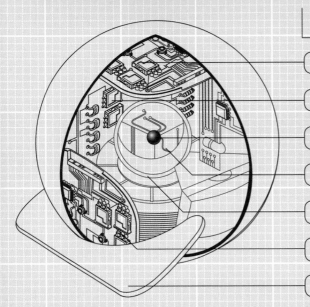

- Dedicated graphics coprocessor
- RAM bus
- Spherical crystalline silicon microchip
- Ionic wind cooling system
- Ionic wind containment sphere
- Dedicated vector geometry coprocessor
- Heat sink

Round processor: Sayle Enterprises developed an innovative new method of manufacturing microchips. The traditional process involves etching circuits onto layered wafers of silicon, making a dust-free environment essential. This means that microchip factories – or foundries – are expensive to build, maintain and upgrade.

At the heart of the round processor is a vacuum, contained by a shell of crystalline silicon. The printed circuit is on the inside of the silicon: the gold electrical connectors are driven through the shell to the outer surface, where they connect to the motherboard.

At no stage in the process is the circuitry exposed to air, thus eliminating the need for a sterile environment; the processor is consequently significantly cheaper to manufacture.

Virus delivery system: Powering up the Stormbreaker releases the virus from its compartment in the LCD panel. The trigger mechanism decompresses the gas canister in much the same way as an aerosol, forcing the virus out through the pressure-activated mesh. Droplets of R5 are diffused into the atmosphere with a powerful spray, covering a 160-degree arc up to ten metres from the screen.

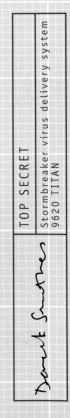

TOP SECRET

Stormbreaker virus delivery system
9620 TITAN

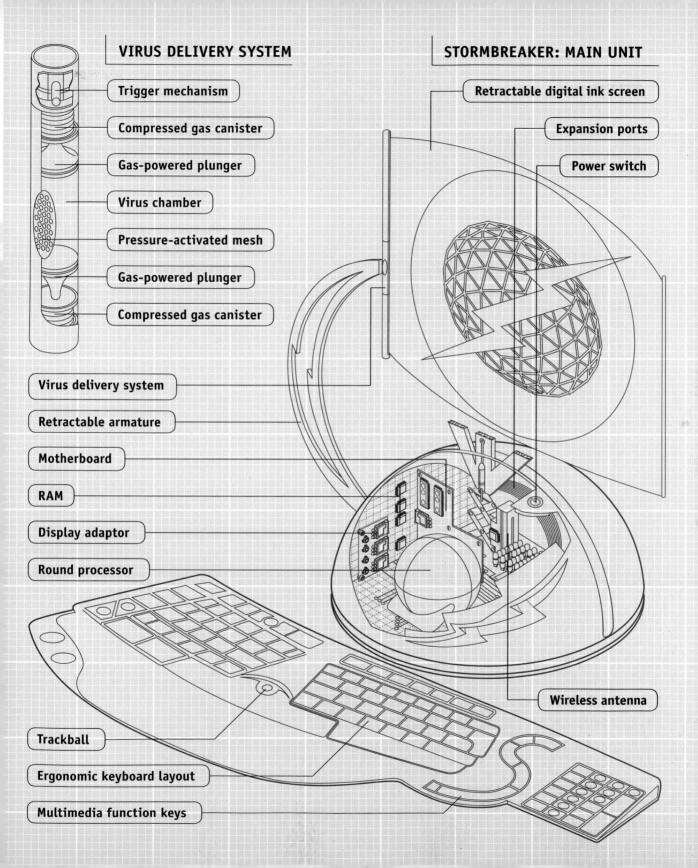

VIRUS DELIVERY SYSTEM

- Trigger mechanism
- Compressed gas canister
- Gas-powered plunger
- Virus chamber
- Pressure-activated mesh
- Gas-powered plunger
- Compressed gas canister

STORMBREAKER: MAIN UNIT

- Retractable digital ink screen
- Expansion ports
- Power switch

- Virus delivery system
- Retractable armature
- Motherboard
- RAM
- Display adaptor
- Round processor

- Wireless antenna

- Trackball
- Ergonomic keyboard layout
- Multimedia function keys

THE R5 VIRUS

This lethal strain of the smallpox virus was intended for use on millions of schoolchildren by Herod Sayle.

R5 is a genetically engineered version of the smallpox virus *Variola major*. Throughout the twentieth century, smallpox was responsible for as many as 500 million deaths; despite the disease only being moderately infectious, around 20 to 40 per cent of those infected die from it.

Thanks to a rigorous campaign of vaccination, smallpox was officially eradicated by 1980 – although small stocks of the virus still exist in laboratories. One such sample was stolen from a Geneva research facility in 1996 by the terror group Scorpia.

The R5 strain was engineered to include the immunosuppressant gene IL-4, which removes the protection given by a vaccination. It is estimated that 99.6 per cent of those infected by this strain would die from it.

In 2001, two hundred litres of weaponized, aerosol-ready R5 was produced in a Scorpia lab and sold to billionaire industrialist Herod Sayle. The virus was transported to Port Tallon in Cornwall on a Han Class nuclear submarine stolen from a Chinese shipyard by Yassen Gregorovich and refitted with sonar-absorbing stealth technology. Sayle intended to use the R5 virus to revenge himself on British schoolchildren. Computer simulations run by MI6 indicate that had the virus been unleashed, millions of children could have been killed within a week.

Genetically modified: The R5 virus was altered for maximum destruction.

TOP SE

PLAN DRAWING: CHINESE HAN CLASS
404 SSN SUBMARINE

Detailed cutaway of the vessel used to
transport the R5 virus to Sayle Enterprises.

MI6 DATA FILE: YASSEN GREGOROVICH

Full biography of the deadly assassin.

MI6 DATA FILES

Classified information on Herod Sayle and his associates.

HEROD SAYLE

Herod Sayle was born in Beirut into a family of sixteen. His parents struggled to support such a large family, particularly when his father's barber shop went out of business, and during Herod's formative years he and his family lived in three small rooms in a tenement building.

As a young boy, Herod was small and undernourished, with no education. But his life changed dramatically when, at the age of seven, he saved the lives of two American tourists in an extraordinary way. While walking along a street in downtown Beirut, he saw a piano falling from the fourteenth-storey window of a hotel: it was being lifted into the building by crane and the cables had slipped. Herod threw himself at a passing couple and knocked them aside as the quarter-tonne instrument smashed to pieces on the street beside them. The grateful Americans were millionaires, and they took an immediate interest in the scruffy, barefoot child. Within a few months Sayle was enrolled in a top north-London boarding school; he barely saw his parents again.

Sayle did well academically and his grades won him a place at King's College, Cambridge, where he continued to excel; a first-class degree in economics was the ideal springboard for Sayle's career in industry. He began by raising enough capital to buy a struggling commercial radio station, which he built up into one of London's most popular and successful media. From there, Sayle moved into the record business and the blossoming computer software market. By this time he was already a millionaire many times over; but the demons that had driven him ever since his escape from the slums of Beirut were not satisfied.

Sayle wanted nothing more than to belong. He soon found that his money could not buy him the respect of London's wealthy elite. Everywhere he went, he was laughed at behind his back by people who thought he was a vulgar man who had made his money too recently -- and with too much effort -- to be part of high society. He was ridiculed in the gossip columns, denied UK citizenship, snubbed by private members' clubs, even as his companies thrived and his millions doubled and redoubled.

Before the advent of the Stormbreaker computer, Sayle Enterprises had been a major player in the manufacture of computer components and peripherals, so it was no surprise when the Stormbreaker was announced. What WAS surprising was the

incredible new design of the machine, and above all Sayle's gesture of generosity towards his adopted nation: every school in Britain was to be given one. The prime minister seized the opportunity to associate himself with the project -- especially as it now became clear that he and Sayle had been classmates at the age of fifteen, in that very same boarding school that had been chosen by Herod's benefactors.

Sayle had been mercilessly bullied at school. His background, his size and his near-illiteracy had instantly made him a target, with the future PM his chief tormentor. Over the years that followed, his resentment and hatred drove him to the edge of madness, and by the late 1990s he was determined to wreak his revenge. By then Sayle had made a number of contacts in criminal organizations, and in 1999 he began to look for sources of biological warfare materials.

His efforts brought him in contact with Yassen Gregorovich (file no. 442), a Russian assassin and agent of the terror syndicate Scorpia (file no. 2416-F: Scorpia). For the sum of £140 million -- a substantial slice of Sayle's private fortune -- Gregorovich secured a stock of the genetically engineered R5 virus. Over the period that the virus and its delivery system were being incorporated into the Stormbreaker computers, Yassen oversaw security at Sayle's Cornwall factory complex.

The date for the Stormbreaker launch was set at 1 April 2001. A special ceremony was arranged at the Science Museum in London, at which the prime minister would throw the switch that would bring all the computers online at once -- and activate the deadly payload concealed within their casing. Millions of schoolchildren would die within days of exposure to the computers -- and Herod Sayle's long-awaited revenge would be complete.

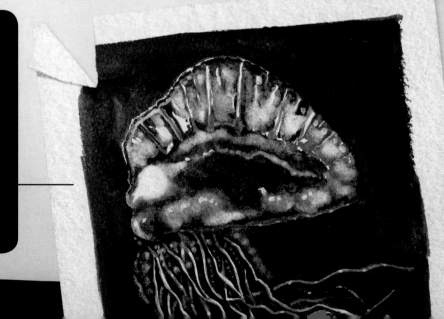

Physalia physalis: Sayle admired his pet Portuguese man-of-war so much that he commissioned its portrait. Following a dispute about the fee, the artist apparently emigrated to South America, leaving no forwarding address.

MR GRIN

REAL NAME: Sean Green

Sean Green was half of the successful circus act The Brothers McBlade.
He and his partner, Jimmy Logan, toured widely with Lloyd's Circus for ten
years, demonstrating great skill in knife-throwing.

One Saturday evening in 1987, Green was performing in his home town of
Maidstone for the first time. It was also the first time his elderly mother
had seen his act. The finale involved Green and Logan catching knives in their
teeth -- a spectacle that usually brought the house down. But at a critical
moment, Green was distracted by his mother waving from the front row. The
spinning knife caught Green in the mouth, causing massive facial injuries.

He lost much of his tongue and required 160 stitches to his cheeks. Plastic
surgeons did their best to minimize the damage, but Green's face was to be
marked for ever by two long, twisting scars, transforming his expression into
a parody of a grin.

The accident permanently affected the balance of Green's mind. After a short
stint back at the circus performing as "the Gruesome Mr Grin", he quarrelled
with both Logan and his employers, and finally walked out. The following month,
Logan's body was discovered in a disused quarry south of Cardiff, with nine
knives embedded in his back. Green was the prime suspect for the killing,
but the police did not have enough evidence to make a case and he was never
charged.

Mr Grin, as he now preferred to be known, was approached soon afterwards by
Nadia Vole (file no. 221) and offered the post of valet and bodyguard to Herod
Sayle (file no. 588). He worked for Sayle for twelve years, also qualifying
as a pilot. MI6 and Interpol suspect Mr Grin of being responsible for several
unsolved murders committed during this time, each one in the vicinity of Sayle
Enterprises' facilities both in the UK and overseas.

NADIA VOLE

Nadia Vole began her career in the Bundesgrenzschutz, Germany's federal police force. A brilliant but unpopular officer, Vole's excellent arrest record was marred by repeated accusations of brutality and corruption. Although no formal charges were ever brought against her, Vole was eventually taken off active duty.

Vole left the Bundesgrenzschutz in 1985 and took on a role as security consultant to a subsidiary of Sayle Enterprises in Leipzig. Three years later she moved to the UK and took over responsibility for press and public relations, working directly for Herod Sayle (file no. 588). Although Vole held a valid diploma in communication theory from the University of Bremen, no students or lecturers from the college recall her attending any lectures -- or in fact remember her at all.

Vole's work for Sayle was largely based around counter-espionage; her PR cover enabled her to keep a close eye on all information entering or leaving the company. It was almost certainly Vole who detected Ian Rider's activities when he posed as a security guard in order to investigate Sayle Enterprises. She was killed by multiple stings from Sayle's pet Portuguese man-of-war when the terrible fate she had devised for Rider's nephew, Alex, backfired.

The walls have ears: Herod Sayle's mansion was rigged with hidden microphones, monitored by Nadia Vole. Here she has concealed a bugging device in a leather-bound notebook.

AT POINT BLANC RANGE

Dr Grief and Point Blanc Academy

POINT BLANC: THE BEGINNING

Research by MI6 brought to light a possible link between three suspicious deaths.

MEMO

From: John Crawley, Section 9

To: Alan Blunt (Chief executive), Mrs T. Jones (Deputy chief executive)

Cc: Psychological profiles (Section 17)

Briefing document 598/559

Subject: Point Blanc Academy, Grenoble

In my recent memo (242/915) I drew your attention to an Orange Code alert from our Overseas News Monitoring division. They had remarked upon three unlikely deaths that had taken place in as many months, as outlined here:

GENERAL VIKTOR IVANOV

Former KGB agent, now director of the SVR and close to the president. Killed when his motor launch, "The Kremlin Lady", inexplicably blew up in the Black Sea. Ivanov had no known political enemies.

ROBERT MERRICK

Australian newspaper magnate and multimillionaire. Owner of "The Sydney Globe", "The Perth Chronicle", "The Adelaide Express" etc. Choked on a chicken bone in a restaurant in Brisbane. Note: Merrick had been a vegetarian for the past six years.

MICHAEL J. ROSCOE

Chairman of Roscoe Electronics, USA, and -- until his death -- the tenth richest man in the world. Killed when he stepped into a lift shaft on the sixtieth floor of his New York office. Due to a mechanical defect, the lift had failed to arrive. No reason has yet been found for this bizarre incident.

The ONM division, in their task of searching for links between strange or unlikely world events, have discovered what may or may not be a coincidence: ALL THREE MEN HAD SONS AT THE SAME SCHOOL IN SOUTH-EAST FRANCE, CLOSE TO THE SWISS BORDER. Point Blanc Academy styles itself as a finishing school for the children of wealthy and successful parents. It is run by a South African, Dr Hugo Grief, formerly a lecturer at the University of Johannesburg. Fees are a hefty ten thousand pounds a term.

Note: background material held on Grief comes from various sources, not all of which are reliable. He may have been associated with the notorious Cyclops Institute in Pretoria, which reportedly used human guinea pigs in a series of medical experiments in the mid 1960s (see file CI/P/223(B)).

Grief is also associated with Eva Stellenbosch (file no. 297), one of the most brutal members of BOSS, the South African Bureau of State Security, who left the country with him twenty years ago. We have asked Interpol to send us any information they have on the couple since their arrival in France.

Given the power and influence of the families associated with Point Blanc Academy -- and following the three unexplained and possibly suspicious deaths -- it is our recommendation that MI6 Special Operations should take a closer look at this so-called "finishing" school.

Might this be another opportunity for Alex Rider? Rider surprised us all with his expert handling of the Stormbreaker business (see file no. 6324-N: Stormbreaker). In retrospect, it seems likely that Ian Rider had been preparing him for this line of work throughout his young life -- as things have turned out, we have been handed a unique and invaluable resource.

We understand that persuading Alex to take on a second assignment may not be easy. But the age range at Point Blanc is 13+ and if some lever could be found to put him into place, nobody would be better suited for an initial Search and Report operation.

Comments?

*s Sir
John
*y he
*ice,"
*unk
*ank
*ut
*in

*id
*en
*nd
*he
*ot
*ly
*g
*n
*n

School to "guarantee" good behaviour

By Rachel Parker

It's the answer to a parent's prayers – an exclusive boarding school that guarantees to solve the problem of badly behaved teenagers. Point Blanc Academy, an isolated former sanatorium high in the French Alps, opens its doors for the first time this week, with fees as dizzying as its surroundings. But for £10,000 per term, the principal, Dr Hugo Grief, promises to turn his pupils' lives around.

"Many children of wealthy and powerful parents experience difficulty coming to terms with the discipline and routine of traditional schooling," Dr Grief claims. "Our approach combines those virtues with the best modern scientific practices. It is an entirely new way of doing things and I am confident that parents will not complain about the results."

The academy is open only to boys aged between thirteen and fifteen – the ideal time, according to Dr Grief, for his intervention to work.

Electron*
falls to *

Michael J. Rosco*
Electronics, has *
York offices, p*
tigato

THE DEATH OF MICHAEL J. ROSCOE

A holographic projector system lay behind the death of the American billionaire.

The untimely death of Michael J. Roscoe in April 2001 at first appeared to be a tragic accident. MI6's investigation revealed that it was in fact murder; responsibility for the killing was eventually claimed by the Gentleman – one of the highest paid and most successful contract killers at large in the world today.

The Gentleman has been active since 1990, and MI6 are no nearer to discovering his identity than they were then. He is a master of disguise, and deadly in many forms of armed and unarmed combat, although he prefers to kill with booby traps and poison. He always sends flowers to the families of his victims (black tulips are his favourite). His fees start at $100,000 and may go as high as $250,000, depending on the job required.

The Gentleman has taken credit for fifty-three killings in total, including those of Jaspar Norton, the Chicago organized crime boss; Natalya Kintsurashvili, the Georgian oil heiress; and Michael J. Roscoe, the electronics billionaire (see files 3233-U: Jackal; 1228-G: Beluga; and 9771-P: Gemini). He has worked for the Iraqi and Colombian intelligence services as well as the Russian mafiya and other international crime syndicates.

6

Electronics king falls to his death

Michael J. Roscoe, the billionaire CEO of Roscoe Electronics, has been killed in a fall at his New York offices, police have confirmed.

Investigators revealed that Mr Roscoe appeared to have stepped into an empty elevator shaft, falling sixty stories from his office. He was pronounced dead at the scene.

"This has all the hallmarks of a tragic accident," said Lieutenant Mark McGavigan of the NYPD. "We're currently working on the assumption that there was a catastrophic elevator malfunction."

Shocked employees at Roscoe Towers were questioned by police and given the rest of the day off.

Roscoe, 54, was the founder of Roscoe Electronics, one of the world's "Big Three" consumer electronics manufacturers. Listed as the world's tenth richest person, his personal fortune is estimated at $14.2 billion.

Police are still trying to contact Roscoe's son, Paul, 14, at his boarding school in the French Alps.

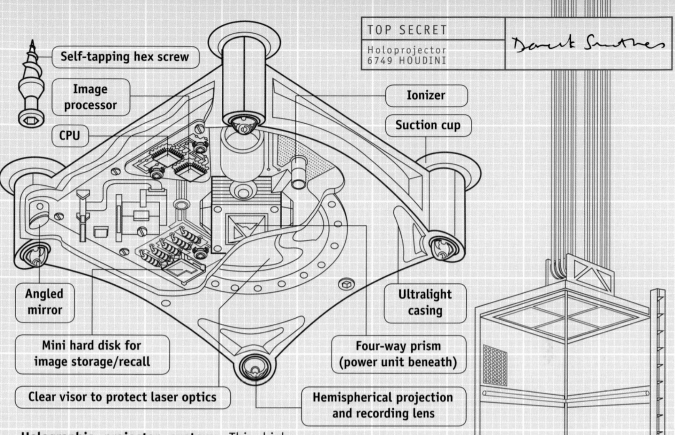

Self-tapping hex screw

Image processor

CPU

Ionizer

Suction cup

Angled mirror

Ultralight casing

Mini hard disk for image storage/recall

Four-way prism (power unit beneath)

Clear visor to protect laser optics

Hemispherical projection and recording lens

Real lift

Projector

Projection

Holographic projector system: This high-resolution video projector uses the principles of holography to produce a clear, detailed image on the walls of the lift shaft.

First, a series of detailed photographs of the real lift are taken using fibre-optic cameras built into the four angled mirrors in the outside casing. The projector is bolted onto the lift's underside. When the unit is switched on, a hologram pattern is generated on the reflective liquid crystal surface of the prism inside it. Laser beams are then bounced off the display, which causes the reflected light to be diffracted. The interference patterns from each beam are directed onto the walls by a series of mirrors, forming an extremely sharp and realistic image. A distorted image of the floor of the lift is projected on the walls of the shaft in such a way as to create the optical illusion that it is present. An air ionizer is used to produce the lightphase changes that help fool the eye – rather like a mirage.

The whole system needs careful calibration and requires forty-five minutes to make it operational.

POINT BLANC ACADEMY

This glossy brochure was sent to five hundred of the world's most influential families over two decades. Competition for places was high.

Welcome to the Academy at *Point Blanc*

Point Blanc Academy is a unique school that is much more than a school, created for boys who need more than the ordinary education system can provide. In our time we have been called a school for "problem boys", but we do not believe the term applies.

There are problems and there are boys. It is our aim to separate the two.

The Academy

Set high in the French Alps, far from the distractions of urban life, Point Blanc offers its students a unique and wholesome environment.

Built in 1857 as a home for eccentric rubber tycoon Louis Fouché, the man responsible for its distinctive architectural style, it later became a hospital. Today the building has been thoroughly renovated, with learning facilities that are second to none.

The classrooms are equipped with the latest technology and an extensive range of textbooks. There is no syllabus that our staff cannot teach, and no exam in which our pupils cannot be prepared to excel.

Included in the west wing are a gym, games room and music room. Use of radios, televisions and personal computers is restricted.

With many sons of high-profile parents enrolled at Point Blanc, security is of the utmost importance – and something of which we are very proud. The only access to the Academy is by helicopter, and an extensively trained security team works around the clock to keep our pupils safe.

The Staff

Point Blanc's teaching staff is small but well qualified. With no more than ten students admitted at any one time, we feel the Academy offers a family atmosphere.

Dr Hugo Grief, the founder and director of Point Blanc Academy, combines many years of educational experience with a deep and compassionate understanding of the needs of troubled teenagers. His track record at Point Blanc is excellent, with remarkably consistent exam results from his students.

Assistant director Eva Stellenbosch shares the teaching duties with Dr Grief. Responsible for the smooth running of the Academy, she also attends to the students' emotional needs. Physical fitness, discipline and respect for authority are central to Ms Stellenbosch's teaching style.

Security chief and former special forces lieutenant Markus Heftig oversees the hand-picked team of thirty security personnel.

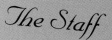

"Since coming to Point Blanc my life has turned right around — thank you, Dr Grief."

"It just goes to show that the old-fashioned ways are the best. My son is like a different person."

"I almost can't believe the change in my son... Thank you, Point Blanc Academy!"

SCHOOL OR PRISON?

Situated high in the French Alps, the academy was massively renovated under the instruction of Dr Grief – and securely guarded.

En souvenir de Point Blanc

Point Blanc Academy was a chaotic, asymmetric building perched on the side of Point Blanc mountain. Far above civilization and accessible only by air, it was perfect for Dr Grief's Gemini Project.

The biochemist took no risks when it came to security – as well as having an alarm system installed throughout the castle he had sentries armed with Belgian FN MAG machine guns posted on all the towers, with two more guards permanently on standby in the valley at the bottom of the mountain. The politicians, industrialists and minor royalty who sent their teenagers to the academy believed these measures to be for the boys' protection. Little did they realize that they merely enabled the genetic engineer to conduct his disturbing experiments away from prying eyes.

TOP SECRET

FLOOR PLANS: POINT BLANC ACADEMY

Diagram based on plans unearthed at the close of the Gemini Project investigation. Annotated by MI6 with specifics relating to Alex Rider's stay at the academy.

CLONING DATA: ALEX RIDER

Medical notes made by Dr Baxter and his team as they prepared to replace Alex Rider with a clone.

BLACK RUN

Alex's escape down Point Blanc was certainly less than conventional.

Makeshift snowboard: Alex Rider took to this treacherous slope on a snowboard fashioned from a domestic ironing board. He removed the legs of the board and sheered off part of the metal bed to form a nose. While the aluminium base was a far cry from the low-friction, abrasion-resistant P-tex favoured by pro-snowboarders, the steepness of the descent enabled Rider to freeride over the uneven ground. In the absence of highbacks and straps he tied his feet to the board's underside with strips of material, which offered flexibility but little protection for his ankles.

1. Infrared googles

2. Bulletproof ski suit

3. Cut-down ironing-board legs

4. Curved front of board

5. Rider's foot tied to underside of board with strips of bedsheets

Black run: Drawn from notes from the Interpol forensic investigation and the testimony of witnesses, the diagram opposite shows the path taken by Rider from the grounds of Point Blanc Academy into the valley below.

1. Descent begins here, near the disused ski jump.

2. The two pursuing snowmobiles catch up with Rider.

3. Snowmobile #1 crashes into a tree and explodes.

4. Rider and Snowmobile #2 are launched into the air. Rider strikes the snowmobile, sending it out of control.

5. Snowmobile #2 crashes, disabling its rider.

6. Two security staff from the academy wait here, in an unmarked grey van. A machine gun is aimed at Rider as he approaches.

7. Rider launches himself off a mound of snow and lands on the tenth wagon of a passing goods train.

8. The track curves, and Rider is thrown off. He hits a wire fence and is knocked unconscious.

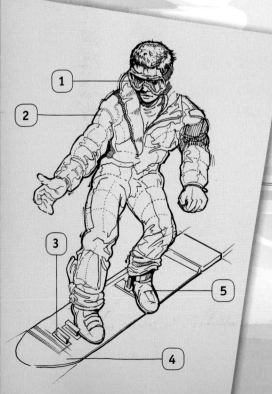

MI6 DATA FILES

Classified information on Dr Grief and his associates.

DR HUGO GRIEF
REAL NAME: Johannes de Leede

Grief first came to the attention of MI6 in 1963 under his real name, Johannes de Leede. A brilliant biochemist and a passionate supporter of the South African government, he rose to the post of minister for science at the early age of 26.

De Leede also held a senior post in BOSS (Bureau of State Security), one of the most feared and ruthless secret police forces in the world, where he was known to be active in chemical and biological weapons research. His goal was to create a disease or poison that would affect only the black population. There is some evidence that he experimented on live humans (see file no. 3452-X: Project Coast).

In 1980, following a series of high-profile scandals, BOSS was removed and replaced with the National Intelligence Service. De Leede knew it was likely that investigators would uncover his theft of government money, and so made plans to escape. In 1981 he used his remaining contacts within the NIS to help steal a final sum in bearer bonds from the South African government; the exact amount is not known but is thought to have been in the region of £100 million. De Leede then faked his own death in a light-aircraft crash and fled to the French Alps with a small group of trusted allies. The NIS never discovered either that de Leede was responsible for the theft or that he was still alive.

Changing his name to Dr Hugo Grief, de Leede set up Point Blanc Academy in a mountain-top mansion once used as a lunatic asylum. From this base he continued his research into genetic engineering throughout the 1980s. Somatic cell nuclear transfer -- the technique used to create Dolly the sheep in 1997 -- works by replacing the nucleus of a human egg cell with genetic material from a donor. The egg is stimulated with an electric shock and begins to develop into a person who will be genetically identical to the original donor: a clone. To date, SCNT has not been officially tested on humans; the failure rate is high and many scientists believe that the process causes genetic damage and shortens the clone's life span. Dr Hugo Grief took pains to keep his research unofficial. He worked alone at Point Blanc, using human tissue acquired in a variety of gruesome ways; an industrial-sized microwave, the size of a large van, was used to turn evidence of his failed experiments into ash. In 1987 -- ten years before Dolly -- he finally perfected his technique, and the Gemini Project (file no. 9771-P: Gemini) was born.

The academy attracted pupils from many of the world's most powerful families. The teaching methods were old-fashioned and highly effective, and school equipment was state of the art. The fees were astronomical. Grief funnelled his profits into upgrading his laboratories and installing a comprehensive medical suite into the academy's upper floors. He also bought property, including the Hotel du Monde in Paris. A private army of mercenaries, drawn from the German special forces, was hired at vast expense to protect the pupils -- and to discourage curious visitors.

The families of Grief's charges were stunned by the vast improvement in their children's behaviour and schoolwork. Boys returned from the Alps with nothing but praise for the teachers who had turned their lives around -- and if their parents noticed something strange about the transformation, they were more often than not too pleased to quibble. Only Michael J. Roscoe, Robert Merrick and General Viktor Ivanov were dissatisfied. Their bizarre and untimely deaths raised few questions in the media; MI6, on the other hand, resolved to investigate.

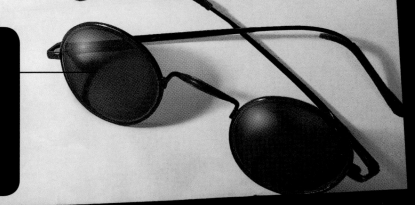

Rose-tinted spectacles:
Dr Grief's interest in genetic engineering was first sparked by his own hereditary illness. His eyes were unusually sensitive to bright light and he wore red-tinted glasses at all times.

EVA STELLENBOSCH

REAL NAME: Eva Viljoen

Eva Viljoen joined BOSS in 1972, at the age of 21. Her talent for cruelty and intimidation soon attracted the attention of her superiors, and for the next three years she carried out missions of assassination, terror and espionage against "enemies of the state". MI6 became aware of her when she was suspected of the kidnapping and murder of an agent in Johannesburg, code name Trefoil. It seems likely that Viljoen was responsible -- cigar burns on the corpse suggested the use of her favourite interrogation technique.

In 1975 Viljoen was assigned to Johannes de Leede (later Dr Hugo Grief) as his bodyguard and helicopter pilot, at his personal request. Grief was also interested in Viljoen's other qualities. An MI6 report, dated 1980, states that: "Eva Viljoen has changed beyond all recognition since she began guarding de Leede. She has always been a fitness fanatic, but in the last five years she has become almost monstrously muscular and athletic. Over this time, she has won the South African weight-lifting championships every year; if she were allowed to compete in the men's competition, I think she might very well still win." Photographs from this time show a noticeable change in the bone structure of Viljoen's face. It is likely that Grief had, for once, found a willing subject for his experiments.

Viljoen assisted Grief in his thefts throughout the late 1970s and followed him to France in 1981, changing her name to Eva Stellenbosch, after her home town. She took up the post of assistant director at Point Blanc Academy and oversaw the security for the Gemini Project (file no. 9771-P: Gemini).

WALTER BAXTER

A brilliant plastic surgeon, Walter Baxter was of central importance to the Gemini Project (file no. 9771-P: Gemini). He altered the faces and bodies of Dr Grief's clones to make them look like the children of the wealthy and powerful, and did it so successfully that it was almost impossible to tell them apart.

Baxter's career as a Harley Street consultant came to an end in 1996 after he was discovered to have altered the features of a Serbian war criminal on the run from the intelligence services; he had become involved with organized crime in order to pay off his huge gambling debts. Before Baxter could be put on trial, he disappeared from the UK, possibly with the help of Eva Stellenbosch.

Once his part in the Gemini Project was completed -- a job which paid him $1 million -- Baxter asked Grief for more money to keep silent. Grief shot him. It is quite possible that Grief would have killed him anyway: Baxter was not a reliable man.

Room thirteen: Baxter's task was made easier by the academy's ownership of the Hotel du Monde in Paris. Room thirteen was in fact a cleverly arranged hydraulic lift connected to his scanning lab, in which the initial evaluation of the boys was made.

1. Room entrance
2. Observation port
3. False floor
4. Hydraulic plungers
5. Photographic array
6. Bank of computers
7. Instrument trolley
8. Lift buffer

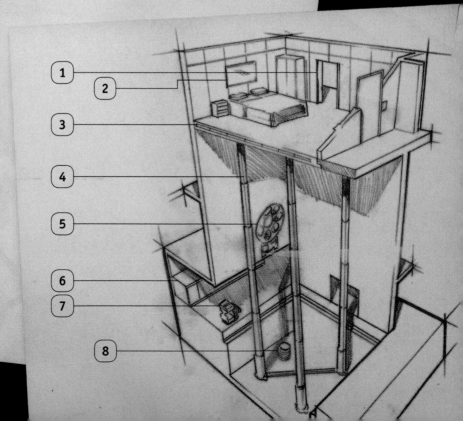

NUCLEAR FAMILY

General Sarov and the Murmansk Incident

From the office of Joe Byrne
Deputy Director Special Operations

What follows is an update on the situation regarding Cayo Esqueleto (Skeleton Key) and a possible recommendation.

As you should all be aware, Skeleton Key is a small island, twenty-four miles long and six miles wide, just off the south coast of Cuba, by which it is owned. The main industry of the island used to be rum but is now high-end tourism – although direct flights from the USA are banned.

At the northern tip of the island is an old plantation house called the Casa de Oro ("House of Gold"), which is home to a man well known to us: General Alexei Sarov, one-time second in command of the Red Army of the former USSR.

Sarov is a fanatical Communist. He lost a son fighting in the war in Afghanistan and left Russia after the collapse of the Berlin Wall. He then moved to one of the few remaining Communist countries and has long been a magnet for Russian dissidents.

Although he is a personal friend of the Russian president, this guy is seriously bad news. He wants to turn back the clock. As he has repeatedly stated, he will do anything to achieve his ends.

We believe General Sarov has recently taken possession of a nuclear bomb.

We don't know what he's going to do with it but we have to find out. The Chief of Staff has ordered me to make this a number one priority. Our brief is as follows: (1) penetrate Skeleton Key; (2) close in on Sarov; (3) find the bomb and, if necessary, terminate with extreme prejudice.

Here's the problem: getting onto the island is not easy. They have world-class security, and previous attempts have ended in fiasco. Most recently, Agents Shepherd and Gerrard entered the capital, Santiago de Cuba, as birdwatchers. What was left of them was washed up off the coast of Miami three weeks later.

The fact is, Sarov is waiting for us. He knows we're coming. He won't let us arrive.

However, we may have a solution. A single agent is suspicious; a pair of agents – a man and a woman – might be able to pass as tourists. But what do they need to put them above suspicion? A kid!

And we may have found exactly the kid we need.

Believe it or not, we've been hearing rumors that British intelligence has used a fourteen-year-old boy on two occasions with complete success. I know it sounds crazy, but we've done some research and it turns out to be true. The kid's name is Alex Rider and his uncle worked for MI6 Special Operations until he was KIA.

I am contacting Alan Blunt (director of Special Operations) to see if we can borrow Alex. We'll line him up with two special agents and they can travel to Skeleton Key as a family on vacation. All the boy has to do is get them through the airport. After that, he can sit in the sun.

Obviously he will have a British accent, but we can work round that. And before you ask – no, there is no US equivalent of Alex Rider. Maybe that's just as well. The American public would go crazy if they thought we were taking a teen out of high school and putting him in jeopardy.

Only the Brits would do something like that!

Joe Byrne

THE TRIADS AT WIMBLEDON

2001's Wimbledon Tennis Championships were notable for the unusual number of unlikely results and the vast sums of money bet on the matches.

The 2001 Wimbledon Championships were highly unusual. Several of the top-seeded players were knocked out in the early rounds by unknown French qualifier Jacques Lefevre. Lefevre had been strongly backed in the sports betting markets of the Far East – as much as $2 million was thought to have been bet on him, at odds of 300–1, to win the tournament. When Lefevre failed to appear for his semi-final match, claiming an ankle injury, he lost the tie by default – and Chinese triad organization the Big Circle lost a huge sum of money.

The organized-crime syndicates known as triads operate in Hong Kong, Macao, mainland China, Taiwan – anywhere with a significant Chinese community. They have existed since the eighteenth century, when they were an underground network dedicated to the overthrow of the emperor. Now they are known for drug-trafficking, people-smuggling, extortion, bootlegging and murder for hire. The attempt to manipulate the Wimbledon Championships – using a modified water cooler to selectively drug players – would have netted the Big Circle $600 million, as well as driving out of business many of the triad's competitors in the world of illegal gambling.

Triads are headed by a Mountain Master, who oversees all the operations run by his organization. Below him are several grades of officer, including the Incense Master, the White Paper Fan and the Red Pole.

JAMIE'S BLITZED!

NUMBER TWO SEED DOWNED BY CRACKER JACQUES!

German hotshot Jamie Blitz crashed sensationally out of Wimbledon on Monday – and says it was the WORST match of his life.

Blitz, beaten in straight sets by French qualifier Jacques Lefevre, was tipped to win easily. "I've never played so badly," said the German ace afterwards. "I can't understand it. I just couldn't get my game going today."

Hapless

Lefevre blasted THIRTY aces past hapless Blitz as the second seed went down 7–6, 6–3, 6–2. "For sure, it was a surprise that Jamie played like he did," said the 22-year-old from Lyons.

Lefevre's shock win has NETTED him a tie with US Open champion Owen Bryant on Wednesday.

prompting delays "John pundits to say he will NEVER The 23–¦ not

JACQUES THE BRYANT-KILLER!

Jacques Lefevre carried on his giant-killing form with ANOTHER shock win at Wimbledon yesterday – and the Frenchman isn't finished yet.

The 300/1 outsider beat world no. 4 Owen Bryant 4–6, 7–6, 6–4, 6–2 at the All England Lawn Tennis and Croquet Club and says: "I'm not afraid of anyone in the draw. If I can get past Jamie Blitz and Owen, I can go all the way."

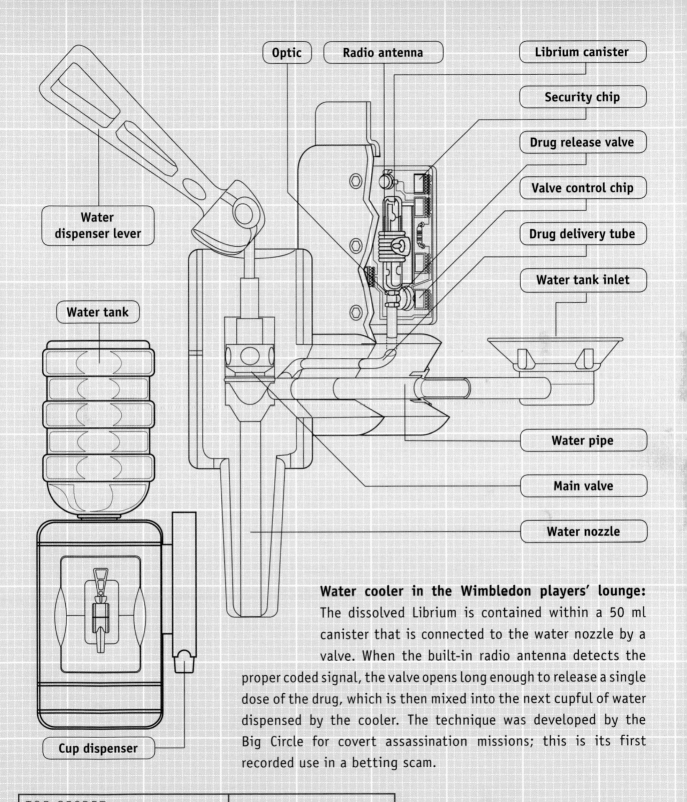

Optic

Radio antenna

Librium canister

Security chip

Drug release valve

Valve control chip

Drug delivery tube

Water tank inlet

Water dispenser lever

Water tank

Water pipe

Main valve

Water nozzle

Cup dispenser

Water cooler in the Wimbledon players' lounge:
The dissolved Librium is contained within a 50 ml canister that is connected to the water nozzle by a valve. When the built-in radio antenna detects the proper coded signal, the valve opens long enough to release a single dose of the drug, which is then mixed into the next cupful of water dispensed by the cooler. The technique was developed by the Big Circle for covert assassination missions; this is its first recorded use in a betting scam.

CASA DE ORO

General Sarov made his home on the Cuban island of Skeleton Key, where he had an old sugar plantation modernized for his purposes.

For almost four hundred years, Cuba was the property of its Spanish conquerors. The colonists set up plantations to grow sugar, tobacco and coffee – lucrative crops which were often farmed by slaves. Conditions were appalling: within a century the original inhabitants of the island had been worked to death, and Cuba began to import Native Americans and Africans.

The Casa de Oro on the island of Cayo Esqueleto was one such plantation. It housed two hundred workers at the height of its success, packed into the filthy and cramped slave house, or *barracón*. The original owner, Alejandro Corrazon, was famed for his cruelty; he would take personal charge of punishing disobedient slaves and is known to have beaten and whipped men and women to death for attempting to escape. Corrazon was himself killed in the slave revolt of 1868 – cornered and torn apart in the *barracón* by the people he had brutalized all his life.

The estate's bloody history did not deter General Alexei Sarov from purchasing it. He fortified the old plantation as if it were a military command post: guard towers manned by elite special forces soldiers

CASA DE ORO: KEY
1. **Electric perimeter fence**
2. *Barracón* **(slave house)**
3. **Sarov's private suite**

4. **Watch tower**
5. **Security office**
6. **Swimming pool**
7. **Stable block**

surrounded the entire island, body-heat detectors and ultra-sensitive microphones were installed at the compound's single entrance, and alarms and spotlights were fixed to the existing buildings.

Sarov and his private staff lived in the main house, an elegant nineteenth-century building complete with original features, including arched colonnades, cascading fountains and marbled courtyards. Beyond the house were the stables, where the general kept his thoroughbred horses, and the old *barracón* itself, which he used for the detention and interrogation of prisoners. The interiors of many of the buildings were extensively modernized: Sarov added video-editing and communications suites as well as a lead-shielded underground bunker for the assembly of nuclear weapons.

THE DEVIL'S CHIMNEY

CIA agents Turner and Troy met their grisly deaths in Sarov's underwater cavern.

1 Ladder to Casa
   de Oro grounds

2 Motion detector

3 Motion detector
   range

4 Disguised titanium
   spikes

5 Hydraulic pistons –
   2000 psi

6 Body disposal system

A natural fissure in the cliffs near the Casa de Oro presented a tempting opportunity for the CIA. While it was almost impossible to enter the compound from the land, a narrow passage led down through the rock into a subterranean cave below. A ladder, installed by smugglers in 1750, provided access to Sarov's property for anybody with the right information – and an advanced scuba course.

However, the Devil's Chimney was not only booby-trapped but also home to the ocean's most fearsome predator: the great white shark. The great white, which can grow up to seven metres in length and weigh two tonnes when fully grown, is a superbly efficient hunter, able to smell a single drop of blood in 4.6 million litres of seawater. Special organs known as the ampullae of Lorenzini give the shark the ability to sense the tiny, electrical fields given off by living creatures; a great white can detect the equivalent of a single torch battery from 1,600 kilometres away.

Its killing power is no less impressive. In a single bite, the great white can devour over fifteen kilograms of meat. Often the shark will bite once and then withdraw to wait for its prey to die from massive blood loss. This may allow a human victim time to get to the safety of a boat or to shore – although it is unlikely they will escape with all their limbs attached...

WARNING: IT IS AN OFFENCE TO BREAK THIS SEAL WITHOUT FULL MI6 AUTHORIZATION

TOP SECRET

CENTRAL INTELLIGENCE AGENCY
CODES AND CIPHERS PAMPHLET
Booklet containing secret methods of communication to be used by field agents when approved communications devices are unavailable. All new agents are expected to learn them.

NUCLEAR WARHEAD

Sarov's nuclear device was designed to cause a meltdown among the nuclear submarines at the Murmansk shipyard. This is how the bomb would have operated.

The essential ingredient of a nuclear weapon is uranium-235, a radioactive metal. The uranium is made into a hollow sphere placed at the centre of the bomb, which is surrounded first with a shell of beryllium, then a pusher shell of steel and finally a shell of high explosive.

When the explosive is detonated, the shock wave is reflected inwards, squeezing the uranium and reducing it to a third of its original size. At this point it becomes supercritical and some of the uranium atoms split, releasing neutrons and a burst of energy. The neutrons then bombard nearby uranium atoms, splitting them and releasing even more energy and neutrons. This creates a chain reaction and causes a nuclear explosion.

The explosive has to be very carefully shaped to direct all the energy inwards towards the uranium core, otherwise the bomb cannot become supercritical and simply fizzles.

General Sarov's plan in the Skeleton Key affair was to detonate a nuclear weapon at the shipyard where the Russian Northern Fleet is located.

Besides the devastation the main weapon would have caused, the reactors in the nuclear submarines anchored there would have melted down, causing massive steam explosions and clouds of radioactive particles.

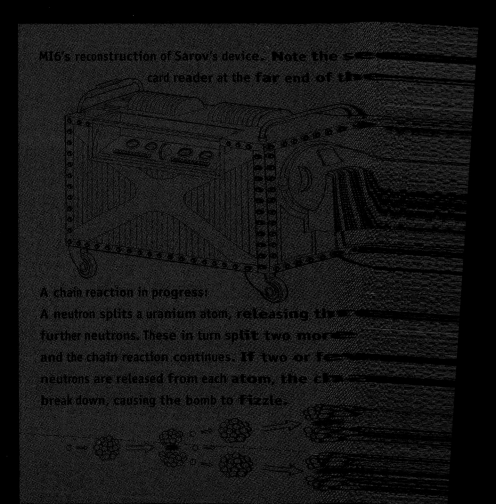

MI6's reconstruction of Sarov's device. Note the ⬛⬛⬛⬛⬛⬛⬛ card reader at the far end of th⬛⬛⬛

A chain reaction in progress!
A neutron splits a uranium atom, releasing t⬛⬛ further neutrons. These in turn split two mor⬛⬛ and the chain reaction continues. If two or f⬛⬛ neutrons are released from each atom, the ch⬛⬛ break down, causing the bomb to fizzle.

A natural fissure in the cliffs near the Casa de Oro presented a tempting opportunity for the CIA. While it was almost impossible to enter the compound from the land, a narrow passage led down through the rock into a subterranean cave below. A ladder, installed by smugglers in 1750, provided access to Sarov's property for anybody with the right information – and an advanced scuba course.

However, the Devil's Chimney was not only booby-trapped but also home to the ocean's most fearsome predator: the great white shark. The great white, which can grow up to seven metres in length and weigh two tonnes when fully grown, is a superbly efficient hunter, able to smell a single drop of blood in 4.6 million litres of seawater. Special organs known as the ampullae of Lorenzini give the shark the ability to sense the tiny electrical fields given off by living creatures; a great white can detect the equivalent of a single torch battery from 1,600 kilometres away.

Its killing power is no less impressive. In a single bite, the great white can devour over fifteen kilograms of meat. Often the shark will bite once and then withdraw to wait for its prey to die from massive blood loss. This may allow a human victim time to get to the safety of a boat or to shore – although it is unlikely they will escape with all their limbs attached...

WARNING: IT IS AN OFFENCE TO BREAK THIS SEAL WITHOUT FULL MI6 AUTHORIZATION

TOP SECRET

CENTRAL INTELLIGENCE AGENCY
CODES AND CIPHERS PAMPHLET

Booklet containing secret methods of communication to be used by field agents when approved communications devices are unavailable. All new agents are expected to learn them.

NUCLEAR WARHEAD

Sarov's nuclear device was designed to cause a meltdown among the nuclear submarines at the Murmansk shipyard. This is how the bomb would have operated.

The essential ingredient of a nuclear weapon is uranium-235, a radioactive metal. The uranium is made into a hollow sphere placed at the centre of the bomb, which is surrounded first with a shell of beryllium, then a pusher shell of steel and finally a shell of high explosive.

When the explosive is detonated, the shock wave is reflected inwards, squeezing the uranium and reducing it to a third of its original size. At this point it becomes supercritical and some of the uranium atoms split, releasing neutrons and a burst of energy. The neutrons then bombard nearby uranium atoms, splitting them and releasing even more energy and neutrons. This creates a chain reaction and causes a nuclear explosion.

The explosive has to be very carefully shaped to direct all the energy inwards towards the uranium core, otherwise the bomb cannot become supercritical and simply fizzles.

General Sarov's plan in the Skeleton Key affair was to detonate a nuclear weapon at the shipyard where the Russian Northern Fleet is located.

Besides the devastation the main weapon would have caused, the reactors in the nuclear submarines anchored there would have melted down, causing massive steam explosions and clouds of radioactive particles.

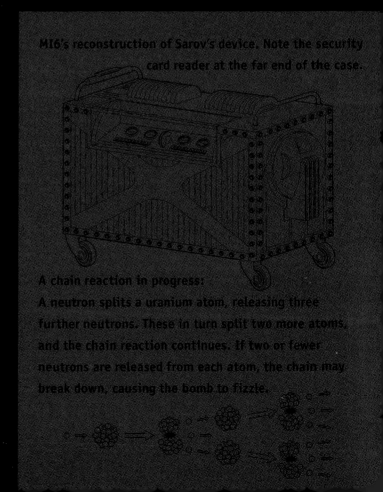

MI6's reconstruction of Sarov's device. Note the security card reader at the far end of the case.

A chain reaction in progress:
A neutron splits a uranium atom, releasing three further neutrons. These in turn split two more atoms, and the chain reaction continues. If two or fewer neutrons are released from each atom, the chain may break down, causing the bomb to fizzle.

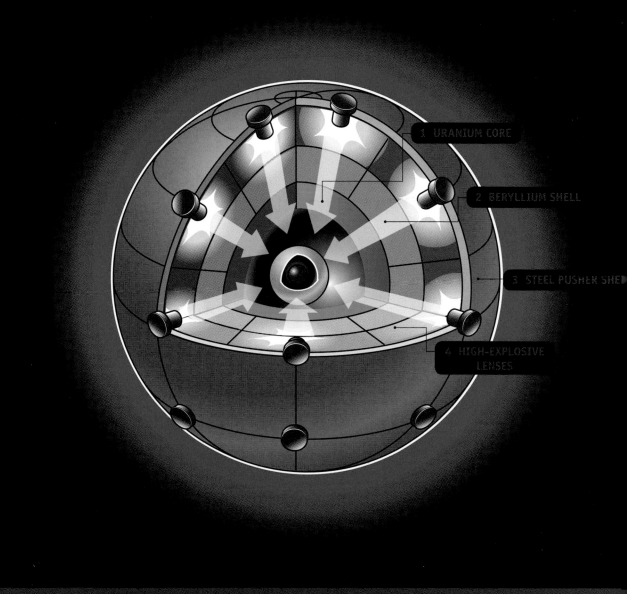

1 URANIUM CORE

2 BERYLLIUM SHELL

3 STEEL PUSHER SHELL

4 HIGH-EXPLOSIVE
   LENSES

The uranium core ❶ has been machined into a hollow sphere. Surrounding it is a shell of beryllium ❷, a stiff, brittle steel-grey metal. Beryllium is used because it tends to reflect rather than absorb neutrons, so fewer neutrons are lost when the core is achieving criticality. Around the beryllium sphere is a steel or depleted uranium shell ❸ designed to help the core hold together during the explosion. Surrounding the steel pusher shell is a complex arrangement of precisely shaped and manufactured high-explosive lenses ❹, calculated to direct the force of the explosion inwards. This explosive is commonly a PBX (plastic-bonded explosive), which has a rigid polymer base. This enables the lenses to be cut to the correct size and shape relatively simply without the risk of accidental detonation.

GENERAL ALEXEI IGOREVICH SAROV

Alexei Sarov joined the Red Army of the Soviet Union at the age of sixteen.
A fervent Stalinist in his youth, he soon proved to be a brilliant soldier.
When the Hungarian Revolution broke out in the winter of 1956, Sarov was called
up as part of Operation Whirlwind -- an overwhelming Soviet force designed to
crush the rebels who had seized Budapest, the capital. The revolt was swiftly
put down, but not before the young private's infantry unit was ambushed by
Hungarian troops. More than half the thirty-strong detachment were killed by
mortar fire and petrol bombs in the first few moments of the surprise attack;
among the dead were Sarov's superior officers. Cut off from reinforcements
and pinned down by Hungarian artillery, Sarov took command, engineering a
miraculous victory against seemingly impossible odds.

Sarov received a field promotion to sergeant and continued to climb the
ranks with unprecedented speed. The Red Army was impressed with his instinctive
grasp of battlefield tactics and urban warfare; the KGB was equally approving
of his dedication to the Soviet cause.

In 1978 Sarov was promoted to general and posted to Afghanistan as a
military adviser. Soon afterwards, a growing rebellion and a palace coup led
the Soviet Union to deploy the 40th Army. In 1979 Sarov was personally involved
in the special forces operation that deposed the president and crippled the
Afghan military.

Sarov rose to become the second in command of the Red Army. When his son,
Vladimir, was killed on assignment in the Helmand province of Afghanistan,
Sarov refused to abandon his troops to attend the funeral.

His glittering career came to an end in 1989 with the start of the collapse
of the Soviet Union. Sarov was disgusted with the path his country was going
down; capitalism had firmly taken root, and a new breed of entrepreneurs was
taking charge. He resigned from the army and left for Cuba, whose old-fashioned
Communist government welcomed him with open arms.

When Boris Kiriyenko came to power in Russia in 1994, Sarov decided that he had to take drastic action to save his country. Sarov had known Kiriyenko since childhood, and although their "friendship" was occasionally useful for political purposes, Sarov had always despised his countryman's weakness and untrustworthiness. Now the most powerful man in Russia was, to Sarov's certain knowledge, a liar and a drunk.

It took Sarov seven years to put his master plan into action. He set up base at the Casa de Oro, an abandoned sugar plantation at the northern tip of Skeleton Key, an island just to the south of Cuba, and recruited the freelance terrorist known as Conrad to run his secret operations. He also made contact with the Salesman (file no. 843) -- the one man he knew could supply him with the vital ingredient his plan needed to make it work. This ingredient was delivered into Sarov's hands by three couriers who later became alligator food: one kilogram of uranium-235.

Red Square parade: General Sarov's troops take part in a military display.

The Order of Lenin: Soviet Russia's highest military honour, awarded to General Sarov in 1979.

CONRAD

ALIASES: Naim Okur; Andon Shabani; Konrad Usupov

Conrad, whose brief but bloody career ended in the Murmansk shipyard incident (file no. 6984-A: Graveyard), was for several years the world's most feared terrorist.

Little is known about his early life. He has been tentatively identified as Naim Okur, the son of a butcher from Istanbul. Certainly Okur seems to fit the bill; at the age of nine, he destroyed his school with a home-made bomb as revenge for being put in detention. Records of Okur's life after this incident have been lost.

The man known as Conrad first surfaced during the Bosnian war in 1993. Initially fighting on the side of the Bosnian Muslims, he deserted and sold his services as a mercenary to the highest bidder. He was in demand: extremely well trained in hand-to-hand fighting, small arms and demolitions, and completely ruthless. Conrad came to the attention of MI6 while commanding a unit of special forces under the control of the notorious warlord Arkan. This unit was heavily involved in acts of "ethnic cleansing", political assassination and sabotage.

Conrad left the conflict in 1994 and started out on his own as a terrorist for hire. With no political beliefs, and operating purely for money, he carried out some of the most devastating bombings of the 1990s. Incidents in the Paris Metro, the Uffizi in Florence and Athens Polytechnic killed over two hundred people and injured hundreds more; at one time Conrad was top on the wanted lists of nine national intelligence agencies.

Holding it together: Following his accident, the terrorist known as Conrad had a record number of pins inserted into his bones.

In September 1998, on his way to plant a bomb at an army base in Elbasan, Albania, Conrad was almost killed: the bomb detonated in the boot of his car while he was driving. Surgeons at a nearby research centre managed to save his life and reattach the body parts that had been severed in the blast. Horribly disfigured, Conrad managed to convince the authorities that he had simply been a particularly unlucky car thief, and just under a year later -- once he was well enough to walk -- he was released. Around that time, many secret services noted that Conrad seemed to have stopped operating and assumed that he had been killed or imprisoned.

Despite his injuries, Conrad remained a deadly fighter, but he began to find it difficult to pass unnoticed: his appearance was simply too grotesque for effective undercover work. However, in June 1999 he was contacted by General Alexei Sarov (file no. 864) and offered the chance to become Sarov's personal assistant, secretary and right-hand man. Conrad accepted. Over the next two years, in addition to his more general duties, he carried out a number of killings and acts of espio-nage in support of Sarov's goals.

Conrad was killed in a confrontation with Alex Rider during the battle at Murmansk, when a powerful electromagnet was activated directly above him. The many metal pins and plates holding his bones together caused him to be flung towards the magnet at great speed; his neck was broken on impact.

THE SALESMAN
REAL NAME: unknown

The smuggler known only as El Vendedor, or the Salesman, came to a violent end in the international waters between Florida and Cuba. His yacht, "Mayfair Lady", exploded and sank with the loss of all hands.

The Salesman was reputed to be able to acquire or dispose of any illegal products. Arms, drugs -- even people -- were bought and sold by his agents and through a network of front companies. The FBI kept him on their ten most wanted fugitives list for fifteen years, referring to him as the King of the Black Market. By the time of his death, his total worth was estimated at $120 million.

His most spectacular coup, and the deal which lead to his murder, was the purchase of weapons-grade uranium. A team of nuclear physicists working at a run-down government laboratory near Vladivostok, Russia, decided they had had enough of scraping by on meagre and infrequently paid salaries. The Salesman bought a kilogram of uranium for $300,000 and smuggled it back to US waters via a container ship.

FROM THE OFFICE OF THE PRIME MINISTER
10 DOWNING STREET, LONDON, SW1A 2AA

From: Mark Kellner, Director of Communications, 10 Downing Street

To: Alan Blunt: MI6 Special Operations

HIGHLY CONFIDENTIAL: Classification Level 1 (green)

Dear Alan,

The Prime Minister has today received an unofficial memo from ▓▓▓▓▓▓▓▓ at the National Security Agency in Fort Meade. This relates to the recent exchange of hostilities at the Russian port of Murmansk and the death of General Alexei Sarov, an army commander in the former Soviet Union.

According to our sources, a British agent may have been involved in this action – and we wonder if you could confirm this ASAP. As improbable as it sounds, there is a rumour that the agent in question may have been unusually young – indeed, it has been suggested that he has not even reached school leaving age. As there is always a danger that this may come up as a question in the House, the PM has asked me to ensure that he is fully briefed.

I hope you are well. My wife and I look forward to seeing you soon.

Yours sincerely,

Mark Kellner

Mark Kellner

MI6
SECRET INTELLIGENCE SERVICE

Dear Mr Kellner,

The events that you refer to (see file: SKELETON KEY) were part of an American operation and did not take place on British soil.

May I suggest that you direct your enquiries to Joseph Byrne at the CIA (Covert Action)? He can be reached via Langley, Virginia, and I am sure he will be happy to cooperate.

Kind regards,

Alan B

Alan Blunt

FROM THE OFFICE OF THE PRIME MINISTER

10 DOWNING STREET, LONDON, SW1A 2AA

From: Mark Kellner, Director of Communications, 10 Downing Street

To: Alan Blunt: MI6 Special Operations

HIGHLY CONFIDENTIAL: Classification Level 1 (green)

Dear Alan,

Nice try, but your rather brief reply neatly sidesteps the facts as I understand them. I am reliably informed that a British agent was seconded to the CIA for this operation and that, incredibly, he was only fourteen years old.

Can you please confirm that the British secret service is now using children (who are not even allowed to vote or buy themselves half a pint of lager) for potentially lethal field operations? I'd also be interested to know how you intend to react if the press get hold of this. THE SCHOOLBOY SPY; MI6 AND THE UNDER-16s; GUNS AND LOLLIPOPS: I can already see the headlines and, frankly, they make me sick.

I repeat – the Prime Minister wants to know.

Mark Kellner

Mark Kellner

PS If this operation did not take place on British soil, how do you explain the death of a security guard, George Prescott, at Edinburgh Airport? Did he somehow manage to shoot *himself*?

Mark Kellner (Office of the Prime Minister)

From: A. Blunt
To: Mark Kellner
Subject: Your query

Dear Mr Kellner,

I'd be interested to know where you're getting your information from. What is the name of this alleged child?

A. Blunt

From: Mark Kellner
To: A. Blunt
Subject: RE: Your query
Status: HIGHLY CONFIDENTIAL – Classification Level 1 (green)

What do I have to do to get a straight answer out of you people? This is weapons of mass destruction all over again.

All right. His name is Alex Rider. As far as I know, you've already used him twice – in Cornwall and then in south-east France. And the so-called midget who smashed through the roof of the Science Museum and shot the PM quite seriously in the hand (he still finds it hard to wave to the public) was in fact the boy in question.

We cannot have British schoolboys being used in high-level international operations. If Rider was killed, it would involve a cover-up on a huge scale. Whose idea was it to involve this child? Where did he come from?

I want that briefing on my desk by 12 p.m. tomorrow.

Kellner

Mark Kellner (Office of the Prime Minister)

From: T. Jones (Mrs)
To: Mark Kellner
Cc: A. Blunt
Subject: Personnel query

Dear Mr Kellner,

Mr Blunt has asked me to reply to your last enquiry. He is currently overseas.

I have contacted our personnel department to see if we can find any record of this Alex Rider and will reply as soon as I have heard from them.

T. Jones (Mrs)

From: Mark Kellner
To: T. Jones (Mrs)
Subject: RE: Personnel query

I know what you're up to, Mrs Jones. But this won't go away. Are you all completely mad? Third World countries use boy soldiers. Britain is not a Third World country – yet. The PM is demanding blood.

MK

MEMO

From: Mrs T. Jones (Deputy chief executive)
To: Alan Blunt (Chief executive)

Mark Kellner called me this morning. He has decided to make no further enquiries into Alex Rider. He has informed the PM that the matter is closed.

Mr Mark Kellner (MI6 surveillance order no. P26/1) photographed leaving a disreputable establishment, 14/02

Maison Va-Va-Voom — Exclusive Nightclub and Bar

POP GOES THE WEASEL

Damian Cray and the War on Drugs

EAGLE STRIKE: THE BEGINNING

MI6 had no choice but to investigate Alex's allegations concerning Damian Cray.

MEMO

From: Mrs T. Jones (Deputy chief executive)

To: Alan Blunt (Chief executive)

Cc: John Crawley, Section 9

Subject: Alex Rider and Damian Cray

I have several concerns regarding the visit of Alex Rider to this office yesterday afternoon.

Alex recently encountered Yassen Gregorovich (see file no. 442) in the South of France. That, I believe, is beyond dispute. Whether Gregorovich attempted to kill the journalist Edward Pleasure is another matter. (NB: Alex has developed a friendship with Pleasure's daughter, Sabina. We are still unsure exactly how friendly they are.)

Alex claims that he has connected the murder attempt to the hugely successful pop singer Damian Cray (real name Harold Lunt: see file no. 530). This seems extremely unlikely.

1.   Both MI5 and MI6 have run clandestine security checks on Cray. He has been wiretapped twice, and between May and July this year all his Internet activities were monitored. He was subsequently given Gold status: above suspicion.

2.   Cray has been a major donor to the current government. At the last election he gave £1 million.

3.   He is about to launch the Gameslayer game system, which will be a huge boon to UK business. A percentage of the profits will go to charity.

4.   He has campaigned all over the world against drugs. Yesterday he met the president of the United States to discuss his work on environmental issues.

5.   Cray was knighted by the Queen, who is known to be a fan of his music. He is loved and respected throughout the UK. The prime minister has stayed at his holiday home in Barbados on several occasions.

It appears inconceivable that Cray is connected in any way to the attempt on Edward Pleasure's life. Moreover, a new French terrorist organization, the CST (Camargue Sans Touristes), has already claimed responsibility for the attack.

It is also true that Rider is only fourteen. How can he be right and two major intelligence organizations be wrong?

However, I do have concerns. Alex Rider has now proved himself to be 100 per cent reliable on three separate occasions. Given his age, he is remarkably mature and level-headed. He claims that he heard Cray's voice when dialling the number he found on Gregorovich's mobile phone. He could, of course, have been mistaken; but it is unthinkable that he would have made it up.

I would therefore like to suggest the following steps for immediate action:

A.   Reopen the files on Damian Cray. Search for any possible connection between him and Edward Pleasure.

B.   Focus on the CST. We have almost no information on this so-called terrorist cell. Why would they have made Pleasure their target?

C.   Tighten security around Air Force One and POTUS. Cray has just met the president: these recent events could be relevant.

D.   Place Edward Pleasure under 24-hour surveillance. We cannot rule out a second attempt.

I am placing this on the agenda for our next Security Council meeting. At the top!

T. Jones

MEMO

From: Mrs T. Jones (Deputy chief executive)

To: Derek Smithers, Covert Weapons Section

PRIVATE & CONFIDENTIAL

Smithers,

I have been informed that the prototype of the Cannondale Bad Boy bicycle with built-in defence mechanisms has mysteriously gone missing from the Chigwell Street laboratory. So far I have managed to keep this extraordinary breach of security to myself. Please could you tell me what you have done with it?

T. Jones

THE PHENOMENON OF DAMIAN CRAY

Cray had a successful and varied career, as these documents attest. No one could have imagined what lay beneath his generous, peace-loving facade.

GAMESLAYER

Our roving reporter Patrick Insole brings you the low-down on DAMIAN CRAY'S next-generation console.

Not content with being a hugely successful pop star and all-round good guy, Damian Cray is bringing out the most exciting next-gen console we've heard of so far: the Gameslayer.

According to the boffins at Cray Software Technology, this will be twice as powerful as the PS®3 and feature graphics technology to die for.

CST is keeping the details under wraps for now, but it has released a concept sketch of the console and announced the launch title. The world will get its first look at the Gameslayer in action at the launch event in Hyde Park next month, where we'll see FEATHERED SERPENT – a 3D third-person adventure title with an Aztec twist and ultra-realistic graphics.

According to Cray, the game's character models look so real, players will feel like they're part of the action. "We did a lot of research on the way the body works, and specifically on the way it reacts to pain," he told *PGW*. "When your character gets hurt, you wince! It's that convincing. You wouldn't believe the lengths my people went to in order to get those routines right. We tested our equipment to destruction."

Gameslayer will hit the shops on 13th August, priced at £299.99. By Christmas, in addition to FEATHERED SERPENT, twelve other games will be available, among them the ...inated MISSILE COMMAND 3000 and BOMB SQUAD.

The spectacular Pleasure Dome to be built in Hyde Park for the Gameslayer launch.

Damian Cray

White Lines

You are invited to

GAMESLAYER
THE OFFICIAL LAUNCH

Come and witness the next revolution in gaming!

19650219

SLAM!

(2:35)

Slam
Love in a cold
(Cray)

CRAYFISH

CRAY

GAMESLAYER

The first game for Cray Software Technology's new console was to be Feathered Serpent, which took gaming to a whole new level.

Gameslayer releases, is replaced by the representation of the player. Movement, facial expression and clothing are all faithfully reproduced.

Cray could have left it at that; however, his creeping madness led him to push realism even further. Many computer games involve injury and violent death, and Cray wanted these to be accurately reflected in gameplay. A series of home-less people, business competitors and criminals were quietly kidnapped and taken to the huge Sloterdijk manu-facturing compound...where they were subjected...against their will in the pain ... reproductions of the sets ... Gameslayer launch ... the bodies

TOP SECRET

CGI VISUALIZATION:
FEATHERED SERPENT

Concept drawings from the studios of Cray
Software Technology used for planning the
set and costumes of Gameslayer's flagship
title, Feathered Serpent.

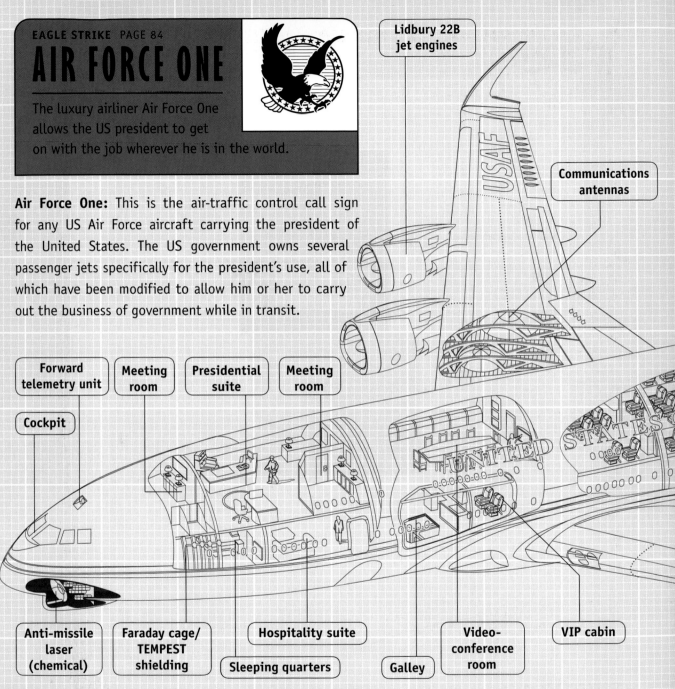

AIR FORCE ONE

The luxury airliner Air Force One allows the US president to get on with the job wherever he is in the world.

Air Force One: This is the air-traffic control call sign for any US Air Force aircraft carrying the president of the United States. The US government owns several passenger jets specifically for the president's use, all of which have been modified to allow him or her to carry out the business of government while in transit.

Lidbury 22B jet engines

Communications antennas

Forward telemetry unit

Meeting room

Presidential suite

Meeting room

Cockpit

Anti-missile laser (chemical)

Faraday cage/ TEMPEST shielding

Hospitality suite

Sleeping quarters

Galley

Video-conference room

VIP cabin

Norland Aerospace won the most recent contract, worth $800 million, to supply two aircraft. The result, the USAF-P12, is a 105-person capacity, triple-deck, four-engined widebody jet crewed by thirty people, including a medical staff and security personnel.

Air Force One contains a full presidential suite comprising a private office, a multigym, a small dining area and sleeping quarters for three people. Presidential aides and Cabinet members stay in cabins near by. Sleeping arrangements for the remaining passengers are also significantly more comfortable than on commercial flights – each seat in the main cabin converts into a single bed.

is equipped with broadcast standard television cameras. The communications system on board is also linked to the military command network, including missile command, allowing the president to run military operations directly from the air.

Air Force One is hardened against electromagnetic pulses and fitted with anti-missile counter-measures, including chaff, flares and a high-power laser fitted to the nose cone. An escape vehicle inside the rear cargo compartment is designed to meet all possible emergency scenarios: a glider coated in stealth materials, it contains emergency parachutes and is amphibious in case of a sea landing.

The plane's range is approximately 9,000 miles, but as it can be refuelled in mid-air, theoretically it can remain airborne indefinitely.

The conference room contains a full video-conferencing system, using a military standard 50 MB per second encrypted satellite uplink. The president is able to address the nation from this room, as it

Communications centre/missile command

Cargo hold

AMERICA

Main passenger cabin

Amphibious escape glider

Radar

TOP SECRET

Presidential jetliner
5687 CHARON

MI6 DATA FILES

Classified information on Damian Cray and Charlie Roper.

DAMIAN CRAY
REAL NAME: Harold Eric Lunt

Harold Lunt was born in north London in 1950 to wealthy parents, Sir
Arthur and Lady Lunt, who had made their multi-million-pound fortune
building multi-storey car parks. At the age of eleven, Harold was
sent to the Royal Academy of Music, where he trained as a singer. His
classmates included the future Elton John.

When Harold was thirteen, his parents were killed in a bizarre
accident. Sir Arthur and his wife had left their Bentley at the top
of their newest car park and were waiting outside on the street to
be picked up by their official chauffeur. The car's handbrake had
apparently been left off; the heavy Bentley rolled across the car park,
picking up speed, and smashed through the low brick wall around the
edge of the roof. The car fell seven floors to the street below, landing
squarely on Sir Arthur and Lady Lunt.

Harold inherited his father's millions, and in 1966 he left England
to travel in India and the Far East. He returned to Britain in 1971,
having converted to Buddhism, and formed a band. Slam! was highly
successful, with two No. 1 singles and a host of Top 40 hits. Lunt gained
a reputation for championing good causes such as environmentalism and
arms reduction. When Slam! played at charity concerts, the tickets were
always printed on recycled paper.

The band split in 1979, and Lunt changed his name to Damian Cray.
His solo career took off instantly: the first album, "Firelight", went
platinum. Over the course of the next decade, Cray won a host of awards
and discs, donating much of the proceeds from his phenomenal sales to
charity. His free concert at Wembley Stadium in 1986 raised £30 million
to help the fight against famine in Africa; the single "Something for the

Children" was the Christmas No. 1, selling four million copies. He also used his high profile to campaign tirelessly against the trade in illegal drugs.

But Cray had also found other ways to change the world. A campaign against an animal-testing laboratory in Bristol succeeded when the lab's head, Professor Milburn, was kidnapped and murdered; his body was found covered in lipstick and mascara, and drenched in perfume. The lab was shut down soon afterwards. Cray had arranged the killing, and the ease with which he got away with it encouraged him to repeat his crime again and again. MI6 can link him to the deaths of fifteen Japanese whalers, found mummified in their own deep freeze, and the entire board of directors of Beckett & Jowell plc, a Yorkshire-based engineering firm involved in the trade in landmines.

His public image as a "living saint" remained untouched by this wholesale slaughter. In 1990 Cray was knighted by the Queen for his network of drug rehabilitation centres offering free treatment to young people.

By now, Cray's musical output had slowed down, with his campaigning and other business interests taking up more of his time. His companies included a television station, a chain of hotels and Cray Software Technology. Cray invested as much as £150 million in this last business, developing the state-of-the-art games console Gameslayer.

The console's design required an enormous amount of computing and engineering expertise, and Cray hired hundreds of highly skilled programmers and electronics specialists to work in his factory complex in Sloterdijk, Amsterdam. Observers also noted the high security at Sloterdijk, with many guards brought in from international mercenary companies to help protect the company's secrets.

CHARLES (CHARLIE) ROPER

For ten years, Charles Roper held a senior position in the US National
Security Agency's cryptanalysis directorate -- otherwise known as Section Z.
(Note that the NSA is the largest and most secretive of the US intelligence
agencies known to be operating at this time; until recently, the US government
did not even acknowledge its existence.) Roper's cryptanalysis section undertook
much of the code-breaking for the NSA's communications surveillance and security
work, and his team of mathematicians was larger than that employed by any other
government or business in the world.

One of the systems designed by Roper's team was the Milstar security locks
for the US nuclear arsenal, used in the "nuclear football" and Air Force One. In
order to launch a nuclear attack, the president must positively identify himself
and present the "gold code" for the day -- a pass code generated by the NSA and
delivered to him by the White House Communications Agency. To maximize security,
the gold code is designed to be a purely random string of numbers.

The Eagle Strike project (file no. 5342-S: Eagle Strike) commandeered by
Damian Cray (file no. 530) was dependent on using the correct string of
numbers for the day of the assault on Air Force One. For several years, Cray
searched for a way to learn it; then Charlie Roper entered the scene.

MI6 operatives are taught the MICE acronym to explain the four basic
reasons why a person might betray his country. M stands for money; many traitors
are satisfied by selling secrets to the highest bidder. I stands for ideology;
the Communist spies who infiltrated MI6 in the 1950s were motivated by their
political beliefs. C stands for coercion; spies may be blackmailed or otherwise
forced. E stands for excitement; few jobs in espionage are particularly
thrilling, and agents have been known to approach the enemy out of boredom.

Charlie Roper was interested in money. As the top jobs at the NSA are held
by senior military officers, and he had never served in the armed forces, there
was no way for him to rise any higher up the ladder -- so he decided to become
rich selling out his government's top-secret code systems. Roper met Cray in
Kuala Lumpur in 1998, having been introduced by professional assassin Yassen
Gregorovich (file no. 442). Cray offered him $2 million for the key to Milstar.

Roper accepted. He managed to introduce a tiny flaw into the random number
generator that fed into the gold code program. With this, and a knowledge
of government computer systems, he was able to map out a way of breaking

into the sequence of mathematical operations that produced the daily code.

Roper needed a tremendous amount of computer power to create a program that could crack Milstar. Cray realized that buying a large number of supercomputers, such as those used at the NSA, would attract too much attention. Instead he announced that he was forming a new company, Cray Software Technology, to develop a state-of-the-art games console. At his new manufacturing complex at Sloterdijk, Amsterdam, he set up a legitimate business producing the Gameslayer console -- and a secret cryptanalysis section run by Roper.

The Sloterdijk team was successful in defeating the gold code locks, and they wrote their decryption system onto a compact flash drive disk that could interface with the computer systems in Air Force One. The flash disk could recover the codes from Milstar within seconds, so the only remaining hurdle was the need for the president's fingerprints; Cray got round this by meeting with the president and obtaining impressions of his prints during a handshake.

Roper's treachery did not go unpunished. His frequent trips to Europe attracted the attention of investigative journalist Edward Pleasure. Pleasure was critically wounded in a bomb attack planned by Yassen Gregorovich and thus removed as a threat, but Damian Cray decided that Roper had become careless. At their last meeting, Roper demanded the $2 million he was owed. Cray lured him into a sealed room and gave him exactly what he requested -- in the form of eight million quarter-dollar pieces. Fifty tonnes of copper-nickel coins were dropped down on the cryptanalyst, crushing him to death.

Loose change: Charlie Roper's new-found wealth weighed heavily on him.

A STING IN THE TAIL

Scorpia and Invisible Sword

SCORPIA: THE BEGINNING

A board report from the terror group SCORPIA provides a glimpse into the acts of Sabbotage, CORuPtion, Intelligence and Assassination from which it takes its name.

1 Remarks by the Secretary, Zeljan Kurst

At the time Scorpia was founded, almost two decades ago, there were many who thought we would not survive; that our goals of sabotage, corruption, espionage and murder for hire would bring the full might of the world's governments down upon us. And indeed we did have powerful enemies. Our former colleagues declared us to be renegades. Established criminal syndicates resented our growing power. Agents were sent after us – highly trained, well-funded killers and infiltrators. Yet we prevailed; we uncovered the spies and assassins in our midst and sent their corpses back to their employers.

Now Scorpia is acknowledged as the most formidable covert intelligence network in the world. Our influence extends to every inhabited continent. We have even conducted operations in the barren polar regions – last year, for example, our commando teams gained access to a former Soviet biological weapons laboratory in the Arctic Circle, where we secured stocks of weaponized haemorrhagic fever virus. The Executive Board sees no credible threat to the continued expansion of our power and resources.

Our primary goal, however, has always been profit, and I am pleased to be able to report another satisfactory year for the Group.

Revenues have increased for the fourth year running: the Group's cash reserves now stand at £262m, with assets of just under £78m – an increase from last year of 13 and 34 per cent respectively. The latter is due to our acquisition of three RA-115 suitcase nukes from the former Soviet Union in Operation Left Luggage, headed by Mr Kroll. Although it is tempting to sell on or use these weapons immediately, our intelligence suggests that the best plan is to bank them for at least five years; we predict a breakdown of international relations during this period, which will inflate their value. The Executive has voted in favour.

Mr Mikato has made progress with our counter-espionage programme. Key members of the Japanese intelligence services have been blackmailed into allowing our agents access to their systems, which has enabled us to monitor efforts to hinder the Group throughout much of East Asia. A similar programme in Germany, spearheaded by Mr Grendel, has yet to bear fruit.

The sum of £30m has been allocated towards Operation Black Box, which is intended to compromise the security of voting machines in the USA. Dr Three will take charge of this important and long-term project on behalf of the Executive. If successful, we envisage being able to manipulate the results of presidential elections for the foreseeable future. Several officials and software engineers have been identified as key mission assets; Dr Three has already begun to exert his considerable expertise to persuade them to cooperate.

Low-level activities continue to be a vital source of income for the Group. Major Yu's snakehead organization and the signals intelligence trading network maintained by M Picoq are performing particularly well. Our Australian member reports that we are now also enjoying a steady stream of cash from our South East Asian opium brokerage.

Recruitment is up; Professor d'Arc is pleased with the current crop of students at Malagosto. His star pupil, code-named Nile, shows exceptional promise and will be assigned high-profile duties in the coming months. Professor Yermalov believes that the Group now employs the most formidable team of assassins in the world; indeed, every contract taken out with Scorpia over the last five years has resulted in the target's death. Our own losses have been minimal.

Finally, Mrs Rothman presents her latest report on Operation Invisible Sword (attached).

Zeljan Kurst

Approved:

Max Grendel	*MAX GRENDEL*	**Dr Three**	*Dr3*
Levi Kroll	*Levi Kroll*	**Julia Rothman**	*Julia Rothman*
Major Yu	*Major Yu*	**Hideo Mikato**	*Hideo Mikato*
Jean Picoq	*J. Picoq*	**#5**	*卌*

INTERNATIONAL ORGANIZATION OF TERROR

Feared throughout the world, Scorpia has carried out numerous atrocities since its conception.
No continent is left untouched.

6 KYOTO, JAPAN

5 WARATAH CREEK, AUSTRALIA

4 AL AYAN, LIBYA

3 INNSBRUCK, AUSTRIA

1 FOREST BAY, ALASKA

2 SAN ANTONIO, BOLIVIA

ASSASSINATIONS

TERRORISM

EXTORTION/CORRUPTION

ESPIONAGE

SCORPIA ACTIVITY LEVELS:

NONE REPORTED ●   LOW ○   MEDIUM ○   HIGH ○

1 FOREST BAY, ALASKA, 1999

Oil was discovered near the Forest Bay National Park in 1998. However, the area was a nature reserve inhabited by two Alaska Native tribes as well as many species of endangered wildlife. Oil companies lobbied the government and argued in the courts to be allowed to build a drilling platform and refinery there, but were denied. A week before the final appeals were due to be heard, an intense fire swept through the pine forests, incinerating much of the plant and animal life and driving the inhabitants from their homes. The area lost its protected status; oil production began in 2000, with sole rights granted to Prosaic Oil plc.

2 SAN ANTONIO, BOLIVIA, 1984

MI6 suspected Scorpia agents of involvement in the 1984 Senate elections. Several candidates stepped aside unexpectedly on the eve of the polls, prompting suggestions that they had been intimidated into dropping out of the race. One, Hector Nalbandian, was killed in a car bombing that also claimed the lives of his driver, bodyguards and two innocent bystanders. Shortly afterwards, the new Senate ordered federal drug trafficking charges against the Lazaro cocaine cartel to be dropped due to lack of evidence.

3 INNSBRUCK, AUSTRIA, 1991

Two MI6 agents attempting to trace the Scorpia member Grigory Yermalov were killed in a bizarre skiing accident near the town of Innsbruck. The men were found at the Seefeld ski resort three days after failing to check in with the Austria station of MI6. The investigation found that the agents had for some reason discarded their skis and wandered off-piste into the forest. Their bodies were found in the wells of soft, powdered snow between the tree trunks; without skis or snowshoes, they had sunk six feet deep into the drift, as if into quicksand. Although no physical evidence pointed to Yermalov, MI6 was certain he had engineered the deaths.

4 AL AYAN, LIBYA, 1983

Scorpia extorted an estimated $20 million from the Libyan government by threatening to poison the Al Ayan water reservoir. A cylinder of a deadly toxin was delivered to Libyan intelligence, with the message that ten more were installed at camouflaged underwater locations at the reservoir. At the time, Al Ayan served almost a million people. With no chance to locate the cylinders in time, the government paid the ransom. Scorpia then transmitted a radio signal to the clamps that held them to the floor of the reservoir. The cylinders rose to the surface of the water and were disposed of safely.

5 WARATAH CREEK, AUSTRALIA, 1992

Scorpia claimed responsibility for the assassination of Jeff Walker, senior officer in the Australian Secret Intelligence Service. Walker was shot on his private fishing boat, *Blowfish II*, while on holiday. The terror group obtained the details of the agent's movements by hacking into his computer. Despite blanket security surrounding Walker's trip, a Scorpia agent was able to hide on the creek bed using scuba gear for twelve hours prior to the victim's visit. Walker was killed with a silenced pistol fired out of the water; his death was not discovered by ASIS until the assassin had escaped.

6 KYOTO, JAPAN, 1994

Scorpia accepted a reported $70 million from a Japanese doomsday cult to carry out one of the world's most terrifying acts of mass murder. They gained access to stocks of miso soup in the distribution warehouse of a leading supermarket chain and contaminated them with a poisonous mushroom. The toxin, one of the most deadly known to man, kills by destroying the liver and has no known antidote. As symptoms only become apparent two to three days after consumption, thousands of people would have been lethally poisoned before anyone was alerted to the danger. The plot was only foiled when a high-ranking cult member turned himself in.

MALAGOSTO

A seemingly deserted island housed the Training and Assessment Centre for Scorpia, where students were taught the arts of stealth, espionage and murder.

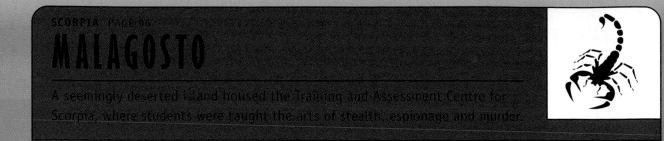

A criminal organization as ambitious as Scorpia needed a world-class training academy. Malagosto, a deserted scrap of land in the middle of the Venetian lagoon, was the perfect location. One of more than seventy islands of varying sizes, Malagosto itself was only half a mile long and lay abandoned.

The island had been a fishing community in the Middle Ages, but was sacked in 1380 in the war with Genoa. The entire population was massacred by the invading forces, and it soon became known as an unlucky, even haunted place. Victims of the plague were sent there to die; later, a monastery and sanatorium were built to minister to the insane.

By the time Scorpia arrived, Malagosto had been deserted for over a hundred years. Julia Rothman handled the transaction, claiming that she intended to build a hotel on the site, but those plans never seemed to progress. Building work did take place on the island, but visitors were discouraged and local officials were quietly paid off.

Scorpia fully renovated the inside of the old monastery, leaving the exterior as dilapidated as before. Accommodation was provided for fifteen students and ten staff, and classrooms were set up to teach everything from infiltration techniques to the use of knives, firearms and explosives. A demolitions training centre and martial arts dojo were hidden away inside the crumbling shell of the sanatorium, with a sophisticated shooting range located on the other side of the island.

Scorpia's Oliver d'Arc was in charge, assisted by a formidable staff whose combined expertise produced a string of killers and criminal masterminds over the years. The academy taught a wide range of fighting techniques, and excellence was encouraged in the ancient ninja and samurai disciplines of stealth and precision. Scorpia agents had to strike undetected until the time came to spread terror and panic – something for which they were carefully trained.

Recruits who could not take the pace, either mentally or physically, had to work hard to defend their place at the training school. It was not uncommon for weaker students to be pitted against their classmates in gladiatorial-style combat – to the death.

MALAGOSTO: KEY

1. Bell tower
2. Classrooms
3. Security office
4. Martial arts training area
5. Refectory
6. Office of Oliver d'Arc
7. Laboratories
8. Dormitories

WESTWAY PILE-UP

A multiple car accident on London's Westway was orchestrated by MI6 to enable Alex Rider to recontact Scorpia without arousing suspicion.

Re-establishing cover for a newly turned double agent is one of the most sensitive intelligence operations. The target organization has to believe that their agent is still loyal – his or her life is at stake. In the recent Westway operation MI6 had to create the illusion that Alex Rider was still loyal to Scorpia. To this end, they faked a major traffic accident on a flyover in central London. The crash was carefully planned by technical specialists in Smithers' R&D team: it involved twenty vehicles, sophisticated radio control equipment and a crew of professional stuntmen and women. The accompanying diagram is a working drawing from Special Operations, showing the planning of the entire sequence.

Alex Rider was in the lead car, accompanied by two MI6 agents and apparently under arrest. As the car approached the elevated section it began to weave back and forth, shunting cars into the crash barriers and off onto the road below. One vehicle's "driver" was in reality a lifelike dummy; an MI6 agent in a car some distance behind was driving it by remote control so that it could be safely launched off the flyover into a nearby house. Traffic behind and below the crash site was carefully managed by plain-clothes police officers to keep innocent bystanders out of harm's way. Rider was allowed to "escape" and re-establish contact with Scorpia. The sheer scale of the "accident", and the destruction it caused, was enough to convince them that he was still working for them – or, at least, not to kill him straight away...

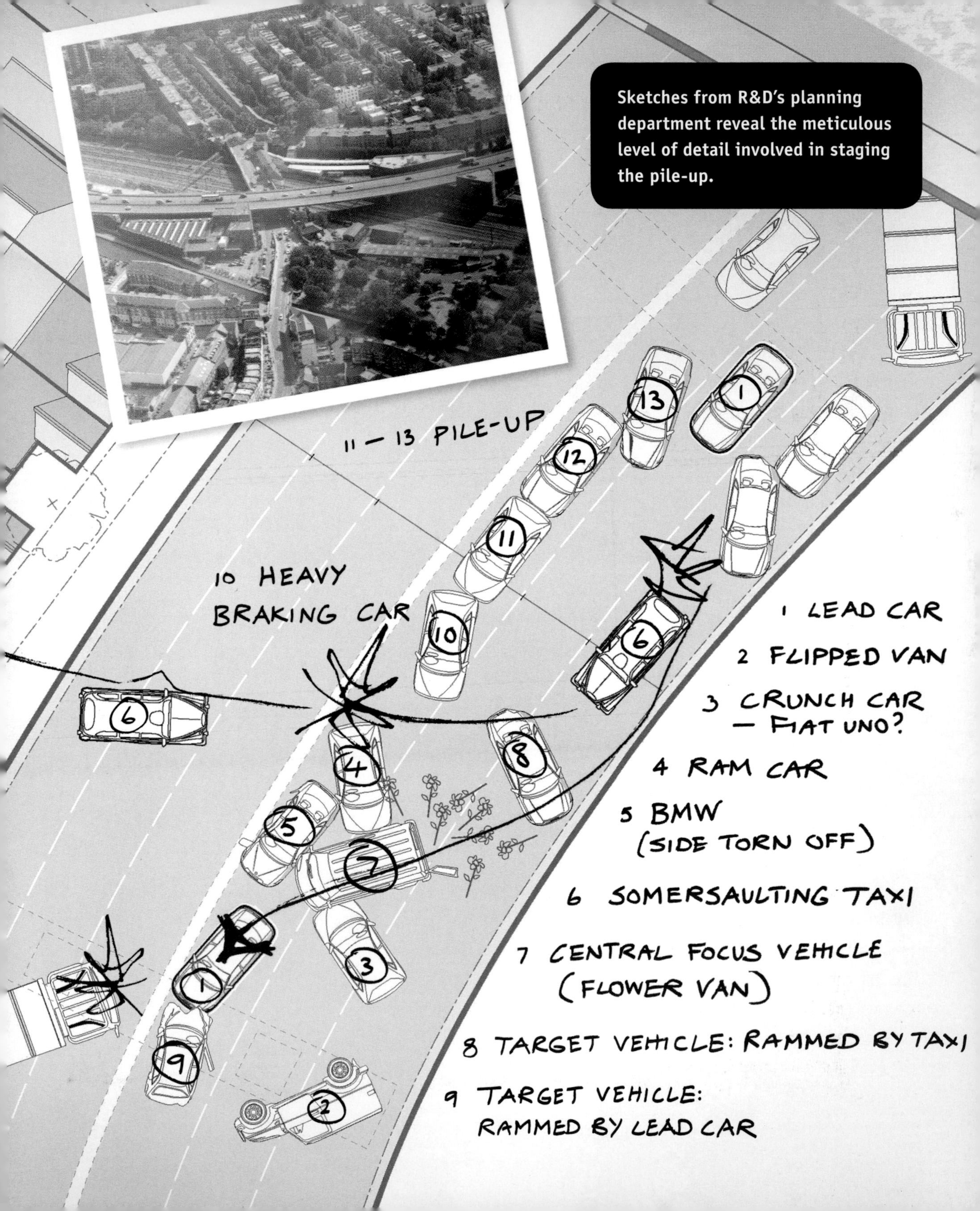

11 – 13 PILE-UP
10 HEAVY BRAKING CAR
1 LEAD CAR
2 FLIPPED VAN
3 CRUNCH CAR – FIAT UNO?
4 RAM CAR
5 BMW (SIDE TORN OFF)
6 SOMERSAULTING TAXI
7 CENTRAL FOCUS VEHICLE (FLOWER VAN)
8 TARGET VEHICLE: RAMMED BY TAXI
9 TARGET VEHICLE: RAMMED BY LEAD CAR

Sketches from R&D's planning department reveal the meticulous level of detail involved in staging the pile-up.

INVISIBLE SWORD

Scorpia's Invisible Sword terror plot was the first to involve nanotechnology: the science of building objects below 100 nanometres – or the equivalent of one eight-hundredth of the width of a human hair. Scientists believe that it is possible to build objects on this scale by putting atoms and molecules together directly. This type of engineering allows for tremendous precision and the ability to manufacture almost unimaginably small and tough machines.

Coal, diamonds and graphite (pencil lead), for example, are all forms of carbon, differing only in the way the atoms are arranged and bonded together. Using nanotechnology, an engineer could take apart coal molecules and construct them as easily as a child playing with building blocks. Cheap materials – even rubbish – could be transformed into diamond buildings. Robots the size of bacteria could be assembled, too small to see with the naked eye but capable of creating objects out of dirt, or of patrolling the human body fixing damage and fighting infection.

But with any revolutionary new technology come grave dangers. The perils presented by nanotech weapons are severe: invisible guided missiles loaded with deadly poison; tiny firearms as deadly as anything available today; artificial plagues. Scorpia's plot relied on gold nanoshells that would release chemicals into a victim's bloodstream once cracked open with a terahertz beam activated by remote control.

But even these threats are not the most nightmarish that scientists have imagined. As nanotechnology progresses, it is likely that self-replicating nanobots will be invented: microscopic machines that can build identical copies of themselves from any appropriate material. If they were to run out of control, a single device could start a chain reaction, duplicating itself thousands of times, each of the copies creating still more, so that in less than two days the mass of self-replicators would weigh more than the earth – devouring the planet and all its inhabitants in the process.

This is known as "grey goo" – the ultimate doomsday nanotechnological scenario. It seems certain that extreme vigilance will be needed; the fate of the world may well hang in the balance.

TOP SECRET

BLUEPRINTS: OPERATION INVISIBLE SWORD

MI6 blueprints of the bomb device at the heart of Scorpia's Operation Invisible Sword, together with its planned launch site, a disused church specially adapted by the terrorists.

MI6 DATA FILES

Classified information on Julia Rothman and Nile.

JULIA ROTHMAN (née EVANS)

Julia Charlotte Glenys Evans spent her early years in South Wales, where her parents were members of the Byddin Rhyddid Cymru, or Free Wales Army, a nationalist terror group dedicated to Welsh independence.

Mr and Mrs Evans were imprisoned in 1965 after a failed attempt to blow up a gas pipeline. Their daughter was brought up in a series of institutions, became involved in crime in her teens and spent her sixteenth birthday in a reform school.

Evans came to the attention of MI5 in 1977, during Operation Spanner (file no. 1320-D: Spanner), an investigation into the sale of naval secrets. At the time, Evans was in a relationship with the junior military attaché at the US Embassy in London; MI5 suspected her of passing information on American submarine movements to the KGB. Before any proof could be uncovered, the diplomat committed suicide.

MI6 continued to suspect Evans of contact with the Soviets, and kept a watch on her for the next three years as she moved around Europe. In 1980, Evans married Sandro Rothman, a multimillionaire construction tycoon from Naples. Two days after the wedding, Rothman fell seventeen storeys from the penthouse apartment of his newest office building: he had leant against the safety rail running around the edge of his private balcony and it had given way. The police concluded that the bolts securing the rail to the building had "sheared through due to metal fatigue".

With her new-found millions, Julia Rothman was able to disappear almost completely from MI6's radar. France's Deuxieme Bureau spotted her in Tangier in 1981, meeting with the ex-Mossad black ops agent Levi Kroll. Then the CIA photographed her in Sicily in 1982 leaving the office of Angelo "il Serpente" Gallo, the head of the most powerful Mafia clan on the island. Soon afterwards, the sensational assassination of an anti-Mafia judge in Palermo was claimed by a previously unknown criminal organization calling themselves Scorpia (file no. 2416-F: Scorpia). Witnesses reported that the machine-gunner appeared to be a woman.

In fact, Rothman was a founder member of Scorpia. She had long since put aside the Communist sympathies that had led her to spy for the Russians, as the USSR was clearly on the way out. Alongside eleven other renegade spies from both sides of the Iron Curtain, she began to direct terror operations around the globe, using her considerable resources and KGB training for financial gain.

At the height of her power, Rothman was in charge of 150 Scorpia agents in fourteen countries worldwide. She communicated with them via a series of cut-outs, dead drops and Internet sites; some agents never even realized they were working for Scorpia. Among the operations overseen by Rothman were the murder of Sam de la Pena, head of MI6's Station P in Lisbon, and the hacking of the Amsterdam Credit Bank's central mainframe, in which a total of £50 million was transferred to over a thousand fraudulent bank accounts in France; the accounts were instantly cleaned out by Rothman's agents.

Rothman's most audacious scheme, code-named Invisible Sword (file no. 6112-I: Invisible Sword), was designed to destroy the "special relationship" between the UK and USA. Scorpia was commissioned by an as yet unidentified multibillionaire to drive a wedge between the two nations, and Rothman conceived the idea of an act of terror on an epic, horrifying scale: an atrocity on British soil which could only be averted by the Americans. Scorpia would make impossible demands of the US president and then carry out its threat.

Using Scorpia funds, Rothman acquired the pharmaceutical company Consanto Enterprises and brought in Dr Harold Liebermann to head up the technical side of the operation. Liebermann had discovered a way to fill tiny nanoshells, gold spheres one billionth of a metre across, with deadly cyanide. These nanoshells were to be injected into London's schoolchildren under the cover of BCG vaccinations and would be perfectly harmless until the gold shells were cracked open by a terahertz beam -- with fatal consequences.

This technology was successfully tested on the England reserve football squad, killing all eighteen members and paving the way for Scorpia's much greater act of terror. When the US government refused to give in to Scorpia's demands, Rothman ordered her threat to be carried out. She would launch the terahertz transmitter array into the skies of London, carried on a camouflaged hot-air balloon, and throw the switch that would kill every fourteen-year-old in the city.

Rothman, however, underestimated MI6's Alex Rider. On Rider's information the SAS stormed the building as Alex struggled with Scorpia agent Nile aboard the hot-air balloon with its deadly cargo. The platform carrying the terahertz dishes was severed from the balloon and fell, ironically, directly onto its creator. Rothman was killed instantly.

Shuriken: This concealed hand-held blade used in the ninja art of shurikenjutsu can either be thrown or used at close quarters: typically for slashing an opponent's arteries.

NILE

REAL NAME (UNCONFIRMED): Nile Griffen

The Scorpia operative known simply as Nile was, for five years, the terror organization's most feared assassin. Details of his career are still uncertain, but records recovered from the personal files of Julia Rothman have allowed MI6 analysts to reconstruct the following information.

Nile was born in 1978 in Britain. He was recruited by Rothman while still in his teens and serving time for grievous bodily harm in a young offenders' institution. Scorpia hackers altered computer files to secure his release, and he was sent directly to the training facility at Malagosto. At the time, Nile was the youngest ever pupil at the school. He became an expert in the martial arts, particularly the Japanese fighting systems.

Nile focused on Bujinkan ninjutsu, the self-defence and espionage art practised by ninja warriors for over eight hundred years. The various disciplines of ninjutsu include taijutsu, or unarmed combat; ninja ken, or sword fighting; shurikenjutsu, the technique of throwing blades; hensojutsu, the art of disguise; choho, or espionage; and shinobi-iri, methods of concealment and stealth. Nile was adept with the entire range of samurai and ninja weaponry, favouring a matched pair of wakizashi or short swords. The swords could be concealed beneath a coat and were specially balanced for throwing. As well as his skill as a fighter, Nile was highly intelligent and completely ruthless; Scorpia regarded him as a prize asset.

The young agent showed remarkable skill and courage on his

early assignments. In 1996 his direct superior Max Grendel sent him to eliminate a low-level Scorpia employee who had sold out to the Italian Secret Service. The double agent was travelling from Palermo to Rome on board a private jet, guarded by six men. Nile entered the baggage compartment of the plane while it was being loaded, and hid until they were an hour into the flight; he then opened an access panel and disabled the cabin pressure sensors. With the sensors out of action, Nile began slowly to lower the air pressure, causing the agents in the main compartment to black out as the oxygen content in the air dropped. He then let himself out of the baggage compartment, suffocated his target and returned to restore all systems to normal. As the agents began to regain consciousness, Nile concealed himself once more, and escaped when the plane landed. The Italians blamed a mechanical malfunction for the loss of pressure and never suspected Scorpia's involvement.

The killing impressed Nile's employees, who had plenty of work for him; Rothman's files record thirty assassinations between 1996 and 2001. Particularly impressive was the fact that no intelligence agency had a photograph or a dossier on Nile; indeed, no agency had any idea of his existence. He used a wide variety of methods, including poison, explosives and edged weapons, but always managed to carry out the hit without being seen -- by anyone except for his victims, that is.

However, Nile had one weakness. At Malagosto it became clear that he suffered from an intense fear of heights: a flaw that prevented him from graduating at the top of his class, and ultimately proved to be his downfall. Nile was assigned to Operation Invisible Sword, his mentor Julia Rothman's audacious scheme to destroy the US/UK "special relationship". When the balloon carrying the terahertz radio array was launched, Alex Rider was on board, working to destroy the equipment before it could be activated. Nile followed, climbing the balloon's ropes even as it soared ever higher above London. His crippling phobia gave Rider the edge in their confrontation, and the assassin fell to his death after being burned by an ignited fuel line.

SPACE INVADER

Nikolei Drevin and Ark Angel

ARK ANGEL: THE BEGINNING

MI6's investigations into billionaire Nikolei Drevin were met with disapproval by the Office of the Prime Minister.

OFFICE OF THE PRIME MINISTER

10 DOWNING STREET, LONDON, SW1A 2AA

From: Mark Kellner, Director of Communications, 10 Downing Street
To: Alan Blunt: MI6 Special Operations

Dear Alan,

Re: Nikolei Drevin and the Ark Angel project

I was very disturbed to learn that your department has recently requested further information concerning Nikolei Drevin, despite the fact that he has been given 100 per cent security clearance by the Ministry of Defence, the Home Office, Special Branch, MI5 and – most importantly – me. It seems that you and your colleagues have been spending too much time in dark rooms. More to the point, were Mr Drevin to learn of this completely unwarranted intrusion into his private affairs he might well decide to pull his business interests out of the UK – with catastrophic results.

Do I really need to remind you that it is thanks to Mr Drevin's involvement – and financial backing – that we are soon to see the first fully functioning hotel in outer space and that it will be flying the British flag? Everyone agrees that space tourism will be the most exciting and important growth area of the twenty-first century. It is a matter of huge national pride that, within months, Ark Angel will be a reality. And it will be ours.

I am well aware that the Americans, in particular the CIA, have been attempting to discredit Mr Drevin. It is hardly surprising. The truth is that we have overtaken them in the space race and they are bad losers. But, despite months of investigation, they have so far come up with no evidence at all. There is nothing – I repeat, nothing – to suggest there is anything amiss in Mr Drevin's business dealings.

These are the facts. Mr Drevin made a fortune in Russia. He began by manufacturing garden furniture and then moved into oil. Yes, it is true that one or two of his business associates were murdered – but he was not even in the country at the time.

He is a man with wide-ranging interests, from property development to football. As owner of Stratford East he has seen his team rise in the Premier League, and I'm looking forward to seeing them take on Chelsea on Saturday.

He has donated hundreds of thousands of pounds to British charities. He has also been a regular visitor to 10 Downing Street, and I recently enjoyed his hospitality on his delightful yacht, the *Crimean Star*.

Finally, you ignore the fact that only this week he has been the target of the vicious terrorist group Force Three, who appear eager to sabotage the launch of Ark Angel. It seems incredible to me that members of this dangerous, illegal organization were able to slip into a London hospital and almost kidnap Mr Drevin's son in the broad light of day! Where were you when this was happening? What action have you since taken? If you were to spend more time investigating Force Three and less time harassing our friends, we might all sleep a little safer.

I hope I have made myself clear.

Yours sincerely,

Mark Kellner

THE MAN IS AN IDIOT.
24-HOUR SURVEILLANCE
TO CONTINUE. A.S.

TERROR EXPERT ASSASSINATED
World authority on eco-terrorism killed by "bomb in mobile"

MAX WEBBER, an internationally renowned expert on terrorism, was assassinated yesterday shortly after delivering a stark warning about the danger posed by extremist environmental group Force Three. Force Three has since claimed responsibility for his murder.

According to sources in the Security Service MI5, Webber's mobile phone exploded as he was making a call, killing him instantly.

Webber had been speaking at a conference in central London, during which he drew the attention of the world's governments to the terror group. "Force Three is the most dangerous terrorist organization in the world today," Webber claimed, "and we ignore its activities at our peril."

80% of human population "must be culled"

Force Three advocates a drastic cull of the world's population in order to reduce the effects of human civilization on the planet's ecosystem. The group's leader and sole spokesman, known only as Kaspar, is said to have directed a recent campaign of bombings and sabotage against logging and mining companies in the Amazon rainforest, and it appears the terrorists are becoming more audacious the longer they evade capture.

The US government raised its terror alert level to Red earlier this year following a report that Force Three had acquired "significant amounts" of weaponized anthrax with the intention of mounting biological attacks on major cities.

Although no such attacks have yet occurred, government sources believe it is crucial to remain vigilant. "Force Three wants to kill four out of every five people on the face of the earth," said one intelligence officer. "It's not about oil, or politics, or religion – it's about mass murder."

ST DOMINIC'S HOSPITAL

The attempted abduction of Alex Rider from St Dominic's Hospital turned into a running battle with Force Three. The teenage spy's efforts to evade capture used all the technology at his disposal.

Alex Rider was perilously close to death. The Scorpia assassin's bullet had deflected off his ribcage and torn his subclavian artery, a major blood vessel supplying the head and arms. Had the bullet struck half a centimetre higher or lower, it would have caused massive and fatal damage to the heart; as it was, the wound would most likely have killed an adult, but Rider was young enough for the artery to respond by shutting down before he bled to death.

The teenager was rushed to St Dominic's Hospital in London; MI6 has an understanding with the hospital management, who frequently provide discreet medical care for injured agents. The surgeons managed to repair the artery and reduce the pressure on Alex's lungs, allowing him to breathe easily again.

However, his recuperation was interrupted by a terrorist attack...

1. Rider witnesses the murder of night-time security guard Conor Hackett by a team of four men, known to MI6 only by the code names Combat Jacket, Steel Watch, Spectacles and Silver Tooth.

2. Returning to his room, Rider swaps the nameplate on his door with Paul Drevin's. The men pursue him.

3. Contact with the kidnap team is made here. Rider shocks one assailant with a cardiac defibrillator: 1,000 volts of electricity causing paralysis of the lungs. He knocks out the second with an oxygen cylinder.

4. Rider lures the third killer to the physiotherapy room, where he has rigged up an improvised catapult from a length of elastic. He uses it to fire a 5-kilogram medicine ball at the man, stunning him.

5. The fourth killer corners Rider in the MRI lab. The MRI scanner uses a tremendously powerful superconducting coil to generate a magnetic field which is used to create a detailed image of a patient's anatomy. However, it can also turn metal objects into deadly missiles; it attracts the man's heavy steel watch, propelling him across the room.

6. Rider is taken by surprise by Kaspar, the leader of the kidnappers and the driver of the getaway van, and is knocked out.

7. Force Three's getaway van.

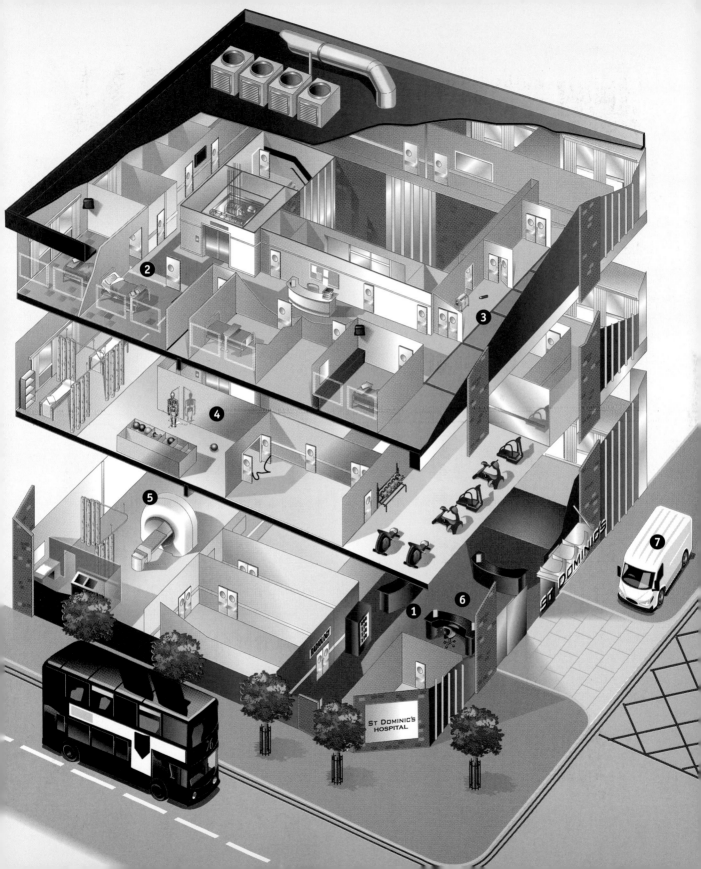

St Dominic's
Hospital

DREVIN INDUSTRIES

Drevin Industries was phenomenally successful; nobody suspected that at its head was the richest criminal in the world.

WHEN THERE ARE NO MOR
WORLDS TO CONQUE
IT'S TIME TO CONQ
THE HEAVEN'

DREVIN: NO CASH CRISIS FOR ARK ANGEL

Nikolei Drevin, Russian billionaire and owner of Stratford East FC, today denied that his audacious space hotel Ark Angel was in jeopardy due to budget and timetable problems.

Mr Drevin confirmed that the hotel, the first of its kind, was running some £300 million over budget – but said it was not a cause for concern. "Some difficulties were to be expected," he said. "This is the most ambitious building project of the twenty-first century."

The government, a partner in the project, also expressed satisfaction with progress to date. A spokesman for the DTI commented, "We're confident that, with Mr Drevin at the helm, Ark Angel will become as much a symbol of modern Britain as the Millennium Dome or the Diana Memorial Fountain."

Shares in Drevin Industries dropped sharply on early trading as the Stock Exchange reacted to the news and to the subsequent announcement by Mr Drevin that he was the subject of a probe by the CIA. The billionaire claimed that it was a routine enquiry and he would cooperate fully. The US government's international intelligence agency refused to divulge why it was investigating Drevin Industries.

Joe Byrne

ED — Message just in from Knight using standard Code-4. Get the map for our assault teams and make sure they look out for Rider.
<u>Worse</u> than we thought.

Joe Byrne

Dear Joe,

Really so exciting to visit this island! I'm now working hard as a personal secretary and learning heaps. I take notes and keep records — what's said in meetings. The weather's hot. Everyone's kind, although at the same time people can always get rattled. We are working night and day to finish things off. The rockets are completely awesome; engineering miracles. The island's heavenly, it really is exquisite. I'm enchanted!

My ankle is less painful... expecting the X-rays soon. Hopefully just a nasty sprain. Otherwise all well. Read your recent letter. I am very sorry Emma isn't doing better. She needs a holiday — France or England maybe.

Love from your friend,

Tamara x.

CIA operative Tamara Knight had to keep in contact with her bosses in Washington DC while she was at Flamingo Bay. This simple letter hides a secret code... Taking the first letter of every other word (starting with the D of "Dear") she passes on vital information.

FLAMINGO BAY LAUNCH CENTRE

The peaceful Caribbean island of Flamingo Bay was the perfect location for Nikolei Drevin's space shuttle launch site.

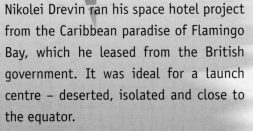

Nikolei Drevin ran his space hotel project from the Caribbean paradise of Flamingo Bay, which he leased from the British government. It was ideal for a launch centre – deserted, isolated and close to the equator.

Two massive gantries were erected to serve the Soyuz-Fregat and Atlas 2AS rockets, which were to carry construction materials and customers to the orbiting Ark Angel. Concrete launch pads weighing over 100,000 tonnes each were created to resist the heat of the main thrusters, and giant water tanks were set up to protect the structure from the 145-decibel pressure of the sound waves produced by the rockets. Although these precautions prevented damage to the launch complex, the local environment was devastated; several species of rare native bird were entirely wiped out in a matter of days. Soon, no more flamingoes flew over Flamingo Bay.

Security, run by Magnus Payne, was tight; watchtowers covered every approach to the island, and the launch site was protected by electric fencing. Checkpoints along the main trails were staffed by armed guards – all of whom had orders to shoot trespassers on sight.

TOP SECRET

CGI VISUALIZATION:
ARK ANGEL SPACE HOTEL

Detailed plan of the space station, created
by MI6 using data retrieved from the Drevin
Industries complex at Flamingo Bay.

MI6 DATA FILES

Classified information on Nikolei Drevin and Magnus Payne.

NIKOLEI DREVIN

At the time of his death, Russian-born Nikolei Drevin was the fourth richest person in the world, with a net worth of $19.2 billion. He was one of many entrepreneurs who became fabulously wealthy after the collapse of the Soviet Union, along with men such as Roman Abramovich and Boris Berezovsky.

However, Drevin's wealth had been acquired under unusually shady circumstances. Drafted into the Russian army in 1974, he soon after joined the military intelligence service, the GRU. In 1982 Drevin became a signals analyst at the KGB, where he helped to run information-gathering operations relating to the criminal organizations of the Far East. It was during this time that Drevin developed contacts with the Chinese triads, the Japanese yakuza and the Russian underworld.

When Communism ended in Russia, Drevin left the KGB and began to invest in business. He first resurfaced as the owner of a small gardening tools manufacturer. The company rapidly eliminated the competition -- the heads of several rival firms either sold their businesses to Drevin at knock-down prices, or disappeared completely. By 1994, Drevin was a millionaire and had sold his factories in favour of playing the stock markets. His second million came about through the shrewd buying and selling of oil shares.

In the mid nineties, Russian president Boris Yeltsin began a programme of privatization. Many of Russia's main industries were still owned by the government, and Yeltsin began to sell them off to private investors. The government was so desperate for cash that incredibly valuable companies were auctioned off cheaply to a handful of rich, well-connected businessmen, who then became even richer selling them on to others.

Drevin was rich and well connected, but not rich enough for the prize on which he had set his sights: Novgerol, one of the largest oil companies in Europe. He needed $80 million to complete the sale, and he had barely a tenth of that. In order to raise the sum required, Drevin approached Russia's fledgling organized crime syndicate, the mafiya; and when they failed to come up with enough money, he brought in the triads and the yakuza. In 1996 the deal went through.

Novgerol shares soared. By 1998 Drevin had paid back his investors with interest, but he realized that continuing his association with them could be even more profitable. He became a banker and broker for a vast range of illegal dealings. In 1999 he engineered the sell-off of a cache of Russian energetics weapons to terrorists, netting himself $40 million in commission, and it is believed that at the time of his death he had opened negotiations with several groups over the sale of Soviet "suitcase nukes": atomic bombs small enough for a single person to carry and operate.

Intelligence agencies and police forces who attempted to investigate the deals found that witnesses and informants rarely lived long enough to testify against Drevin in court. At one stage, an entire St Petersburg apartment block was destroyed by a bomb; over two hundred people were killed. Although the atrocity was blamed on Chechen separatists, many believe it was designed to conceal the murder of a journalist who had stumbled on the links between Novgerol and the Chinese triads.

Drevin's base of operations was his mansion in Oxfordshire: Neverglade. In typical fashion, he had had the building transported stone by stone from Scotland, and rebuilt with twenty-first-century additions. As well as his oil business, he had invested heavily in property and even bought a struggling London football team, Stratford East. Most famously, he maintained a private island in the Caribbean, which was the headquarters for Project Ark Angel (file no. 4211-L: Ark Angel) — possibly the most awe-inspiring engineering project ever conceived. Drevin proposed to build a hotel in space, catering to the super-rich and run in partnership with the British government.

Ark Angel made headlines worldwide, but despite Drevin's outward optimism, the project ran into difficulties. Costs rose sharply, forcing him to dig deep into his personal fortune to fund it. By early 2001, Ark Angel was costing its creator £10 million a day and showed no sign of being ready for at least another eighteen months. Drevin was faced with humiliation and financial ruin; even worse, he learnt that the CIA's investigations into his illegal activities were coming close to the truth.

CONT.

All that glitters: A fragment of the disguised caesium medallion used to assassinate Stratford East FC's star player, Adam Wright.

Drevin took desperate measures. First, he created the terror group Force Three (file no. 3310-K: F3), ostensibly a network of radical environmentalists but in reality a small team hand-picked from his private security force. Force Three carried out a wave of attacks throughout 2001, aimed at "enemies of the planet": car manufacturers, members of the Atomic Energy Commission and oil executives. The next phase of the operation was to establish Drevin himself as one of Force Three's prime targets. The attempted kidnap of his son, Paul, from St Dominic's Hospital in October was followed by an arson attack at one of his London tower blocks and the murder of Adam Wright, Stratford East's star player. Everything was in place for the final act. Drevin proposed to destroy his own creation and blame it on Force Three. A bomb planted on the space station would knock it out of its orbit and send it on a precisely calculated spiral towards the earth's surface. Ark Angel would strike Washington DC with the force of an atomic bomb, destroying the CIA's evidence and allowing Drevin to recoup his losses from the insurance companies. However, Alex Rider, on a CIA-led mission, managed to uncover the plot. US forces stormed Flamingo Bay, and Drevin was killed in a light-aircraft crash as he tried to make his escape.

Eco-warriors: Fake terror group Force Three sent several communiqués like this one, designed to instil fear into their recipients and cause maximum disruption.

F O R C E • 3

To the Governments of the World:

The human race has become a cancer on the face of the earth, polluting, poisoning and exploiting the planet that gave it life.

Today, the planet fought back once more through its agents, Force Three. We are the antibodies of Gaia. Wherever the infection is deepest rooted, we are there, ready to cut it out. There is nowhere to hide.

Max Webber was an enemy of the earth to which he now returns. Many more like him will follow in the weeks ahead.

MAGNUS PAYNE

ALIAS: Kaspar

When Nikolei Drevin (file no. 115) first met Magnus Payne in 1996, the former British SAS officer was serving fifteen years in prison after his mercenary force had been captured during an ill-fated attempt to take over the country. Drevin realized that the man's combat and leadership skills would make him a valuable asset, and paid $1 million to secure his release. Soon afterwards Payne was appointed vice-president in charge of security at Drevin Industries.

Payne's reputation for cruelty and cunning was well deserved. In the years since leaving the British Army he had fought for pay in many of the world's combat zones, killing and torturing enemy soldiers and civilians alike. Many of his former comrades followed him into Drevin's employ; they were, to a man, fanatically loyal and as vicious and brutal as their leader.

When Force Three (file no. 3310-K: F3) was devised, Payne was the natural choice to front it. Drevin believed that the terror group required a fearsome and memorable public face and Payne took his instructions literally: he had a map of the earth tattooed on his face for the role of Kaspar. Psychological profiles of the man suggest a fascination with physical pain, which might account for his willingness to undergo this agonizing and bizarre procedure. When Payne had to appear in public as himself, he concealed the tattoo beneath a latex mask and wig.

Payne worked at a furious pace to establish Force Three as a name to be feared. In six months he carried out seven bombings, five assassinations and three kidnappings, leading security expert Max Webber (file no. 778) to label it the most dangerous terrorist group in the world.

The supposed attempted kidnapping of Nikolei Drevin's son, Paul, was intended to make Drevin appear one of Force Three's primary targets. The fact that they captured the wrong boy, Alex Rider, did not distract them from this goal. Indeed, Rider became convinced that Force Three were aiming for Drevin, and only discovered the truth about Kaspar later, at Flamingo Bay, by which time it was almost too late.

Payne departed for Drevin's space station Ark Angel aboard the businessman's rocket, "Gabriel 7", intending to set off the bomb which would send the station crashing to earth. As the only agent able to fit into the cargo compartment of the Soyuz-Fregat, Drevin's secondary rocket, Rider was forced to follow Payne into space. A deadly confrontation in zero gravity ended with Payne impaled on his own knife. Rider made his escape aboard the Soyuz-Fregat having harmlessly detonated the bomb, and so the brief but bloody career of Kaspar was at an end.

ONCE BITTEN, TWICE SPY

Major Yu and the Snakeheads

SNAKEHEAD: THE BEGINNING

Alex Rider's unexpected arrival in their waters proved timely for the Australian secret service.

To: Harry Forsythe
Department of Defence, Canberra

From: Ethan Brooke
Covert Action Division

STRICTLY CONFIDENTIAL: FOR YOUR EYES ONLY

Dear Harry,

I've now had a chance to study your lengthy dossier, CURRENT ACTIVITIES OF SNAKEHEAD SOCIETIES IN ASIA AND AUSTRALASIA.

I'm totally with you. It's clear that the snakeheads represent a serious risk to our national stability. They're supplying at least half the weapons used by terrorist organizations in South East Asia. They're up to their slimy necks in the illegal drugs trade. And their people-smuggling operations make me sick to the stomach. Only last month, a freight container with sixty-two Afghan refugees was discovered abandoned at Perth; all but two had died of suffocation. How can anyone make money out of such human misery?

I also agree that we need to target Major Winston Yu, who seems to be in control of much of this criminal activity. However, your suggestion that this department has been slow or inefficient is pretty wide of the mark. We've been doing everything we can, but the truth is that somehow Yu has always been one step ahead. In the past six months alone we've lost two of our best men.

You may remember John O'Donnell – you actually recommended him to me. Well, we managed to get him into Yu's snakehead, posing as an escaped felon. He had a perfect cover and he knew what he was doing, but just a month later he was found washed up in Hong Kong harbour. At least, most of him was. We're still looking for his head.

We thought that maybe O'Donnell was unlucky. So we tried again, this time with a highly trained covert agent called Danny Chu. He was fluent in Chinese, a veteran of our special forces with an A* rating from Swanbourne. We set him up as a low-level triad operative with $2.2 million in uncut diamonds which he was supposedly trading for weapons; again his story was watertight. He made contact with the snakehead in Jakarta.

We got Danny back last week. They sent his ashes to us in an airmail envelope. There was a note attached telling us they'd cremated him to save us the trouble. It seems Major Yu has a sense of humour – if you can call it that.

We're not giving up. We're currently looking at Yu's people-trafficking operation, and surely to God we can insert one or two agents into the pipeline – possibly posing as Afghans. Yu may be smart but he can't run background checks on every refugee who buys passage. Once they're inside the organization the agents will be able to gather information. Above all, we need to find out how Yu knows so much about us.

Just one problem. Where do we find two agents who will be totally above suspicion? How do we avoid the mistakes we made with Danny and John? I don't want any more nasty surprises in the morning post.

I'm working on it. I should have a list of candidates shortly and maybe we can meet and discuss it over a pint at Jacksons on George. Your round.

Ethan Brooke.

FROM--DEPUTY DIRECTOR CIA/SPEC-OPS
TO--CAPTAIN USS KITTY HAWK
FOLLOWING SUCCESSFUL OUTCOME
ARK ANGEL AGENT RETURNING EARTHWARDS
PROJECTED SPLASHDOWN
LAT 28DEG 38MIN 24.45SEC S
LONG 155DEG 51MIN 30.76SEC E
REQUEST DIVERT PICK UP SOONEST

ecrypt

"UFO" was meteor, say scientists

■ By Sarah Foster

A display of coloured lights in the sky near Rottnest Island on Thursday has been attributed to meteor activity, say experts at Siding Spring Observatory.

Fishermen from Rockingham and Fremantle reported an object streaking across the sky at around 4.30 a.m., accompanied by a loud sonic boom as it entered the atmosphere. Although some sources attributed the phenomenon to UFO activity, scientists at Siding Spring say a meteor is the more likely explanation.

"We would very much like to obtain a sample of the meteor for analysis," said Dr Steven Ilic of the Anglo-Australian Observatory. "However, based on its trajectory, it's probable that it splashed down in the ocean."

Western A
government
outcome wi
will deliver
The WA
appeal aga
court deci
people nati
square kil
surround
The c
200,000
Claim c
the rema
resolved.
The go
the ruling
ent with pre
Understoo
not happily
"If it didn't
be doing it,"
stand that the
about this is
the state's app
He said th
the law had
get a very

Ops think it's the Ride boy – Navy is on its way. Prepare an alternative mission profile ASAP assigning him to Ash as the infiltration team. This could work out perfectly.

STRALIAN

LIBERIAN STAR

The Indonesian container ship *Liberian Star* harboured more than a few secrets.

A mammoth container ship, the *Liberian Star* is 40 metres across and more than 300 metres from stem to stern: the length of three football pitches. It can carry up to 325,000 cubic metres of cargo packed into thousands of identical shipping containers, which take up the majority of the ship. The thirty-strong crew lives and works mainly in the block towards the stern. Living quarters, the galley and the bridge are located above deck; the lower part of the block holds the diesel engines, which are capable of driving the vessel at up to 35 knots.

Ships like this carry so much cargo that they can become a target for pirates: a typical load might include cars, consumer electronics, designer clothes, foodstuffs and machine parts and could be worth up to $200 million at any one time. Several of the containers on the *Liberian Star* hold more than meets the eye. Two have been modified with false interior walls, creating small compartments for people smuggling: up to forty refugees can be packed into each one, accessed by concealed trapdoors. The overseers of these operations are unconcerned by the discomfort of their unlucky passengers: conditions are hot, cramped and occasionally lethal, and in the event of an inspection by the authorities it is not uncommon for these containers to be dumped over the side.

A third container, kept in the deepest level of the hold, housed the Royal Blue thermobaric bomb.

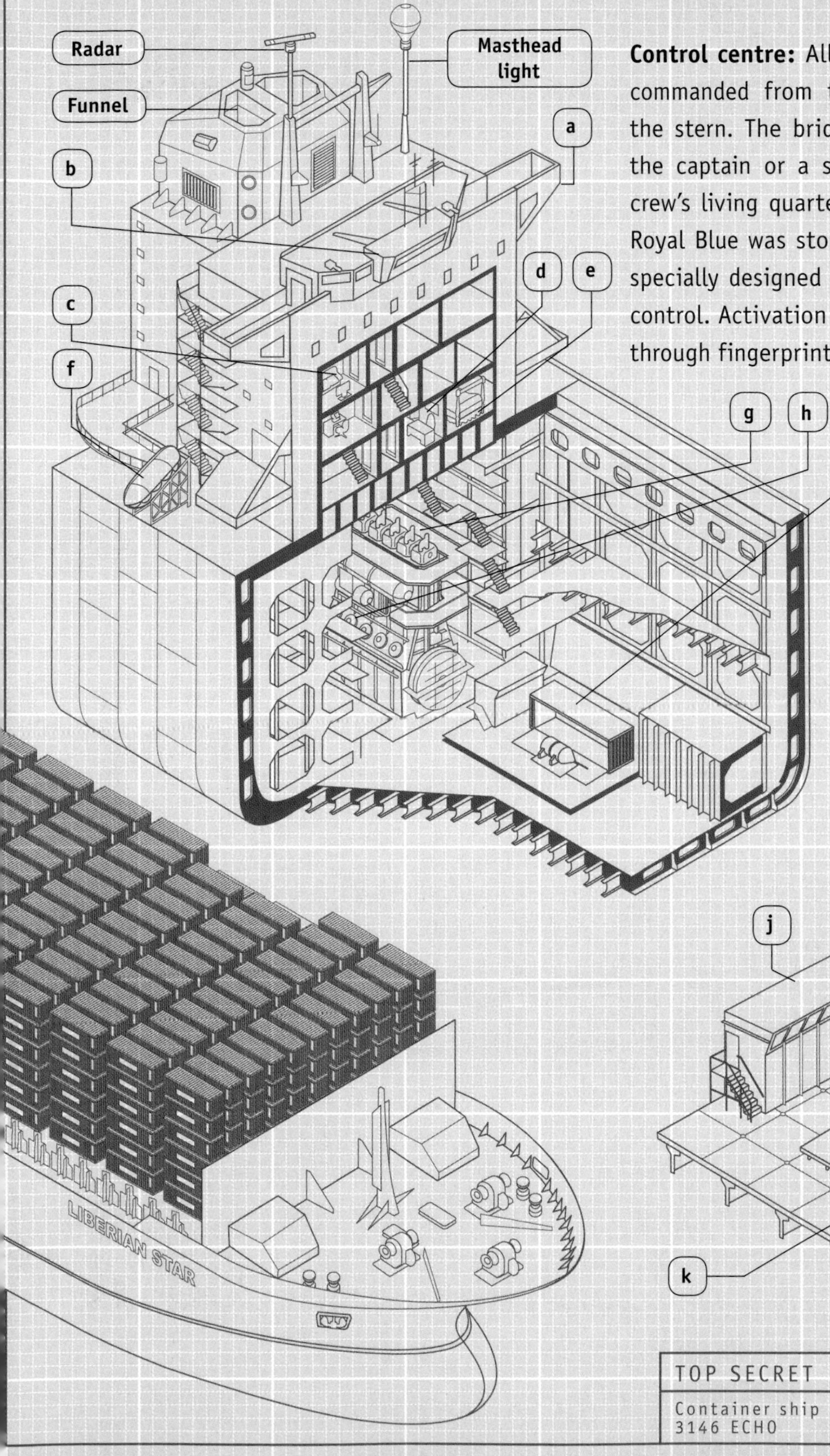

Radar

Funnel

Masthead light

b

a

d e

c

f

g h i

Control centre: All activity on board the ship is commanded from this section, located towards the stern. The bridge is manned at all times by the captain or a senior officer; below it is the crew's living quarters and, below that, the hold. Royal Blue was stored near the engine room in a specially designed container operated by remote control. Activation of the bomb was possible only through fingerprint recognition.

a. Flying bridge
b. Navigation bridge
c. Conference room
d. Stateroom
e. VIP cabin
f. Lifeboats
g. Engine control room
h. Engine room
i. False shipping container
j. Storage observation room
k. Bomb control unit
l. Royal Blue

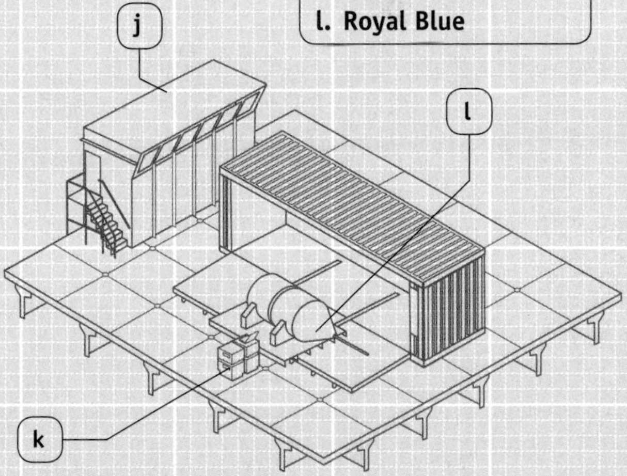

LIBERIAN STAR

j

l

k

TOP SECRET

Container ship
3146 ECHO

JUNGLE HOSPITAL

A secret clinic in the heart of the Australian jungle was the headquarters for a gruesome black-market trade in human organs.

The snakehead run by Major Winston Yu traded in anything and everything illegal. With people smuggling proving such a lucrative business, it was only logical that the gang should move into the harvesting and sale of human organs.

The black market in body parts is highly lucrative: a healthy liver may sell for up to £50,000; corneas are worth £20,000 each; a heart may fetch as much as £1 million. They come from a wide variety of sources: governments have been known to sell off the organs of executed criminals or political opponents; sick children from poor communities have been sent abroad for "treatment", never to be seen again. There have even been reports of tourists waking up after a night in the bars and clubs of a foreign city to find they have been drugged and are now missing a kidney. The trade is extremely difficult to detect – the victims are most often dead and the recipients may not even know how their life-saving transplant was arranged.

The nerve centre of Major Yu's operation was a hospital complex in the Kakadu National Park, an area of wilderness almost half the size of Switzerland. The clinic was hundreds of miles from the nearest centre of population and was surrounded by jungle, accessible only by seaplane or riverboat. Infested with crocodiles, poisonous snakes and biting insects, the park was a natural barrier, blocking any chance of escape.

The Kakadu clinic had a staff of seven, with Dr Bill Tanner in charge. Tanner, a gifted surgeon, had been struck off by the Australian medical authorities after telling a liver transplant patient that $50,000 could guarantee her place at the head of the transplant queue; he was quickly recruited by the snakehead and spent the rest of his career removing the body parts of luckless refugees, kidnapped children and enemies of Major Yu.

HOSPITAL: KEY

1. Jetty
2. Office and administration centre
3. Water tower and generator
4. Radio tower
5. Client accommodation
6. Perimeter fence
7. Hospital block

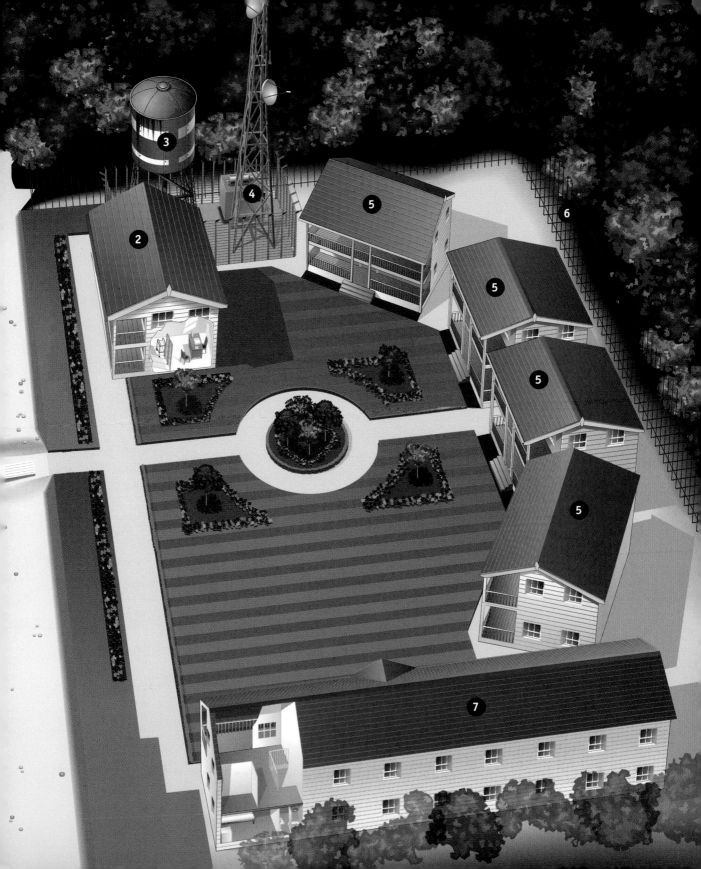

ROYAL BLUE

The delegates at the Reef Encounter summit were entirely unaware of Scorpia's own ideas about how to change the world.

Royal Blue is the code name for the Royal Air Force's version of the BLU-82/B thermobaric bomb developed by the USA. It is the world's second largest conventional explosive, a simple steel shell containing 5,670 kilograms of ammonium nitrate, aluminium powder and polystyrene. The destructive power of the bomb is immense, exceeded only by the Russian-made "father of all bombs" and low-yield nuclear devices.

The BLU-82/B was originally designed to clear helicopter landing zones during the Vietnam War. Approximately the size of a family car, it is usually launched from an aircraft on a sled-like loading pallet at a minimum altitude of 1,800 metres and detonated just above ground level. The accurate positioning of the aircraft is critical to the bomb's success; if delivered correctly it will flatten anything in an 80-metre radius, hence its nickname "daisy cutter".

On an assignment for Scorpia, Major Yu arranged the theft of a Royal Blue from an MoD laboratory near London; he then had it shipped to an oil rig in the Timor Sea, where it was to be detonated beneath the rig's drilling platform.

The location and timing were key. The rig had been constructed over a fault line in the earth's crust; additionally, Major Yu timed the drop to coincide with the alignment of the sun, moon and earth, which would provide maximum gravitational pull. The effective detonation of the bomb one kilometre below the seabed would cause a tsunami that would devastate nearby Reef Island, and with it much of the west coast of Australia.

1. **Steel shell**
2. **Explosive**
3. **Detonator**
4. **Fuse and arming device**
5. **Trigger**

TOP SECRET

CGI VISUALIZATION: DRAGON NINE

Scale drawing of Major Yu's oil rig as envisaged by the Australian SAS; the artist has shown it in darkness, as it would have appeared during the CAD raid.

CGI VISUALIZATION: TSUNAMIS

Diagrams to show the effect of a tsunami on a body of water, used by ASIS to predict the destruction potential of the Royal Blue bomb.

MI6 DATA FILES

Classified information on Major Yu and Ash.

MAJOR WINSTON YU

It is believed to be one of MI6's great failures of recruitment that the service did not recognize the potential of Major Winston Yu.

Yu grew up in the slums of Hong Kong. His mother, Gong Yu, worked as a chambermaid at the Victoria Hotel, where she had met his father, an English businessman who was a frequent guest. Gong Yu saw Britain as a land of power, prestige and opportunity and was determined to send her son there to enjoy a better life -- but that would require a great deal of cash.

Gong Yu was a resourceful woman. She sought out a local snakehead boss, Jimmy Yuen, and offered her services. Yuen agreed to pay her the equivalent of six months' wages to kill a rival triad enforcer, Tung Li -- a man known to drink regularly at the Victoria Hotel's bar. It was simple for Gong Yu to steal a waitress's uniform and poison Li's Martini using digitoxin. Li was pronounced dead from natural causes, and so Gong Yu had completed the first of many contracts with the simplicity and invisibility that would become her trademark.

Over the next two years Gong Yu earned enough money killing for the snakehead to send Winston to public school in England. MI6 can confidently attribute fourteen deaths to Gong Yu over this period, including the audacious firebombing of a Hong Kong police safe house, in which three police officers and one snakehead informant died.

Winston did not at first find England particularly welcoming and he was bullied at Harrow, which he attended from the age of thirteen. MI6 suspects that the fatal hit-and-run accident that befell his chief tormentor, Max Odey, was orchestrated by Gong Yu -- but whatever the truth of the matter, life swiftly improved for Winston after this incident. As he grew up, Yu's love of all things British never wavered, and after graduating from London University he enlisted in the British Army.

Gong Yu died soon after her son graduated from Sandhurst. It is believed that by now Yu knew the truth about the origins of his mother's money; nevertheless, she remained the most important force in his life. In one of her last letters to her son, Gong Yu quoted the Chinese general Sun Tzu, author of "The Art of War": "Be extremely subtle, even to the point of formlessness. Be extremely mysterious, even to the point of soundlessness. Thereby you can be the director of the opponent's fate."

Yu took this advice to heart. Despite his small stature he proved to be an excellent soldier and tactician and was assigned to Military Intelligence. The army began to use him in much the same way as the snakehead had used his mother -- as an unremarkable-seeming infiltrator and covert assassin. Yu took part in several classified operations in Northern Ireland throughout the 1960s (see files code-named Fish Hook, Flashbulb and High Tower).

Major Yu's military career came to an abrupt end in 1970 when he was diagnosed with brittle bone disease. In a regrettable miscalculation, the army transferred him to a desk job at GCHQ, the British government's signals intelligence centre. The prospect of sitting in an office reading intercepted telegrams as his condition grew steadily worse did not satisfy the major. He decided to go into business for himself.

It is unfortunate that MI6 Special Operations did not take an interest in Yu; though he had served the army with distinction as a professional killer, his keen intellect was in many ways his greatest asset. In 1972 he returned to Hong Kong with a stockpile of top-secret documents, reduced to microfilm, concealed in the sleeve buttons of his tweed Savile Row suit. The snakehead that once employed his mother paid him handsomely for them.

By 1980 Yu was second in command of a criminal empire that spanned South East Asia. His snakehead was primarily interested in people trafficking but also smuggled drugs, weapons and counterfeit goods from East to West. During this time, many of the smaller Hong Kong triads and local crime syndicates were brought under Yu's influence -- by force if necessary. In 1982 an Interpol report commented: "Organized crime in the region is now better coordinated and more profitable than in any other part of the world."

But Major Yu wanted more. He became a founder member of Scorpia, providing much of the organization's financial muscle and a vast pool of criminal talent and expertise upon which to call.

Made in England: Yu's obsession with all things British extended to how he took his tea.

ASH

REAL NAME: Anthony Sean Howell

Howell first came to the attention of the secret service when attached to the 2nd Battalion of the British Army's Parachute Regiment ("2 Para"). Ash, as he prefers to be called, had been identified as an exceptionally gifted and intelligent soldier with a natural aptitude for covert operations. One training exercise saw members of 2 Para "behind enemy lines" in the Scottish Highlands, hunted by UK special forces. Ash's unit not only evaded their pursuers, but also captured their command post without the alarm being raised; Ash himself sent a series of bogus messages to the enemy soldiers, leading them far astray of the other 2 Para teams.

Following this, Ash was offered a job with the Special Operations division of MI6; his speciality became field reconnaissance, providing intelligence, communications and combat support for agents on secret missions. An expert in disguise and camouflage and a skilled linguist, Ash could blend into the background in any city on any continent. Over the course of almost five years he worked on assignments in locations as diverse as Panama City, Copenhagen, Aceh, Sydney, Helsinki, Antananarivo, Bordeaux and Kigali -- all without drawing unwanted attention.

He first met field agent John Rider (file no. 176) in Prague, during a mission targeted at a cell of former Czech KGB agents, code-named Kabal. The ex-KGB officers had obtained a stockpile of Soviet weapons, including AT-7 Saxhorn anti-tank missiles, RPD 7.62 mm light machine guns, and B-11 recoilless rifles -- all highly dangerous in the wrong hands. John Rider's cover was as a potential buyer; Ash was running routine surveillance, ready to step in should things turn sour.

The building where the deal was to take place was the Museum of East European Folk Art and Antiquities, once a real museum but now converted into a warehouse housing smuggled and stolen goods, HQ of the Kabal. Ash watched Rider arrive for his appointment through the scope of a Barrett M82 rifle from his camouflaged position on a rooftop half a kilometre away. A passive transmitter in Rider's belt buckle allowed Ash and his team to follow the progress of the meeting without creating any telltale radio chatter.

Rider met with his contact Milan Strasky in the museum's second-floor display area -- once filled with handcrafted Bulgarian peasant embroidery, it now showcased masterpieces of Soviet gunsmithing. The meeting progressed smoothly until a Kabal lookout reported that they had spotted an unmarked van three streets away, equipped with a military-grade radio aerial. News of the arms cache had unfortunately leaked to Russian military intelligence, who had dispatched their own covert operations team to Prague. However, they were evidently less successful than Ash at maintaining cover: the van, containing three Russian secret service agents complete with surveillance equipment, was swiftly petrol-bombed and John Rider's interview took a sudden turn for the worse.

Ash's team watched as Strasky demanded to know whom Rider was working for. When the MI6 agent refused to talk, the Kabal operative drew his handgun. Ash took aim and fired one shot from the Barrett. The .50 calibre round -- capable of penetrating tank armour -- tore the gun from Strasky's hand, disabling him. Rider took advantage of the sudden confusion and pulled an RPD light machine gun from Strasky's sample case, holding off the Kabal security team that immediately rushed to his location and making his escape through the window.

Ash and John Rider became friends. Rider credited Ash with saving his life -- a favour he was later to repay. When Rider got married, Ash was his best man; when John's son, Alex, was born, Ash became his godfather. And when Rider took on dangerous covert missions, he invariably requested Ash as backup. The Mdina ambush (see file no. 3219-K: Malta) was just such an operation, but unfortunately it went badly wrong, leaving four agents dead and Ash himself stabbed in the abdomen by Russian assassin Yassen Gregorovich (see file no. 442).

John Rider kept his friend alive until the ambulance arrived, but it was the death of Ash's MI6 career: he left Special Operations soon after Rider's death and his own demotion to a desk job. Ash later emigrated to Australia, where he continued to recover from the grievous wound inflicted on him by Gregorovich in Malta; he was eventually recruited by the Australian Secret Intelligence Service.

His current operational status is unknown.

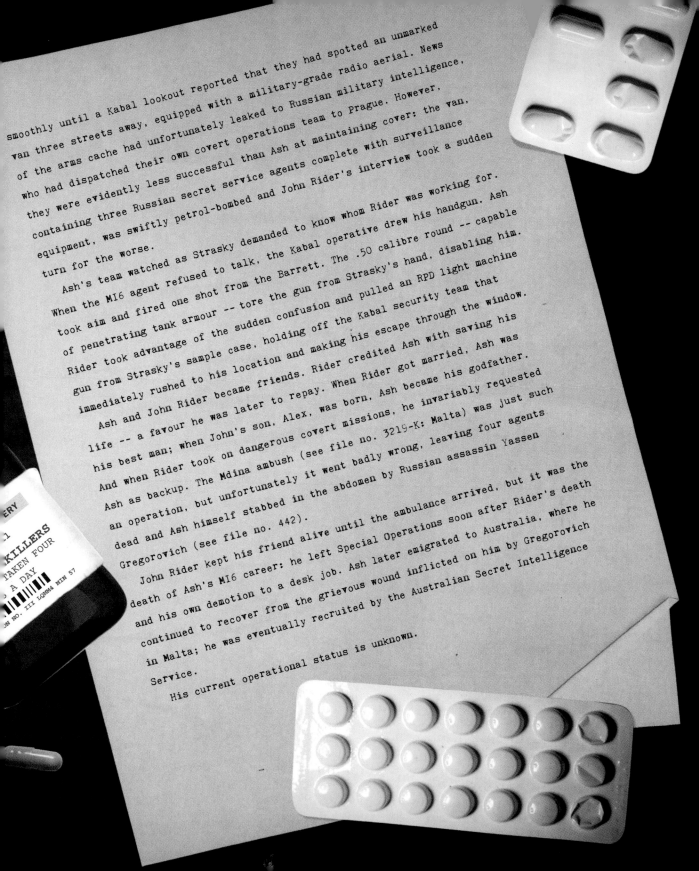

My uncle – Ian Rider – always told me that he worked in international banking. Why did I believe him? Bankers don't usually spend weeks or even months away from home, returning with strange scars and bruises they are reluctant to explain. They don't receive phone calls in the middle of the night and disappear at the drop of a hat. And how many of them are proficient in Muay Thai and karate, speak three languages and keep themselves in perfect physical shape?

Ian Rider was a secret agent: a spy. From the day he left Cambridge University, he had worked for the Special Operations division of MI6. Just about everything he ever told me was a lie, but I believed him because I had no parents and had lived with him all my life and, I suppose, because when you're thirteen years old you believe what adults say.

But there was one occasion when I came very close to realizing the truth. It happened one Christmas, at the ski resort of Gunpoint, Colorado. Although I didn't know it at the time, this was going to be the last Christmas we would spend together. The following spring, Ian was killed on a mission in Cornwall, investigating the Stormbreaker computers being manufactured there. That was just a couple of months after my fourteenth birthday. That was when my entire life spun out of control and I became a spy myself.

Gunpoint had been named after the man who first settled there, a gold digger called Jeremiah Gun. It was about fifty miles north of Aspen, and if you've ever skied in America you'll know the set-up. There was a central village with gas fires burning late into the night, mulled wine and toasted marshmallows, and shops with prices as high as the mountains surrounding them.

We'd booked into a hotel, the Granary, which was on the very edge of the village, about a five-minute walk from the main ski lift. The two of us shared a suite of rooms on the second floor. We each had our own bedroom, opening onto a shared living space with a balcony that ran round the side of the hotel. The Granary was one of those brand-new places designed to look a hundred years old, with big stone fireplaces, woven rugs and moose heads on the walls. I hoped they were fake, but they probably weren't.

For the first couple of days we were on our own. The snow was excellent. There had been a heavy fall just before we arrived, but at the same time the weather was unusually warm, so we were talking powder and lifts with no queues. We started with a few intermediate courses but were soon racing each other down the dizzyingly steep runs high up over Gunpoint itself.

It was on the third day that things changed. It began with two new arrivals, who moved into the room next door. A father and a daughter – she was just a couple of years older than me.

Her name was Sahara. Her dad lived and worked in Washington DC – she told me that he was "something in government" and I guessed she was being purposely vague. Her mother was a lawyer in New York. The two of them were divorced and Sahara had to share Christmases between them.

She was very pretty, with long black hair and blue eyes, only an inch taller than me despite the age gap. She'd been skiing all her life – and she was completely fearless. And, unlike me, she had her own boots and skis. At the time my feet were growing too fast and, as usual, I'd had to rent.

Sahara Sands. Her father was Cameron Sands, with silver hair, silver glasses and a laptop computer that hardly seemed to leave his side. He spent every afternoon in his room, working. Sahara didn't seem to mind. She was used to it; and anyway, now she had Ian and me.

Two more people arrived on the same day as Sahara. They were sharing a smaller, twin-bed room across the corridor. I noticed them pretty quickly because they rarely seemed to be far away, although they never came over and spoke to us. They were both men in their late twenties, smartly dressed and very fit. They could have graduated from the same college. One night – we were sitting at the bar – I suggested that they might be gay, and Ian laughed.

"I don't think so, Alex. Try again."

I thought for a moment. "Are they body-guards?"

"Better. At a guess, I'd say they're American secret service."

I blinked. "How do you know?"

"Well, they're both carrying guns."

"Under their jackets?"

Ian shook his head. "You could never draw a gun out of a ski jacket in time. They've got ankle holsters. Take a look the next time you see them." He looked at me over his brandy. "You have to notice these things, Alex. Whenever you meet someone, you have to check them out ... all the details. People tell a story the moment they walk into a room. You can read them."

He was always saying stuff like that to me. I used to think he was just talking, passing the time. It was only much later that I realized he'd been preparing me. Just like the skiing and the scuba lessons. He was quietly following a plan that had begun almost the day I could walk.

"Are they here with Cameron Sands?" I asked.

"What do you think?"

I nodded. "They're always hanging around. And Sahara says her dad works in government."

"Then maybe he needs protection." Ian smiled. "Let's see if you can find out their names by the end of the week," he said. "And the make of their guns."

But the next day I had forgotten the conversation. It had snowed again. There must have been ten inches on the ground, bulging out over the roofs of the hotel like overstuffed duvets. Sahara and I switched to snowboards and spent about five hours on the chutes, bomb drops and powder stashes at the bowl area high up over Bear Creek. I never guessed that just four months later I'd be using the same skills to avoid being killed by a couple of thugs on snowmobiles, racing down the side of Point Blanc in southern France. But that's another story.

By half past three, with the sun already dipping behind the mountains, we decided to call it a day. We were both bruised and exhausted, soaked with sweat and melted snow. Sahara went off to meet her dad for a hot chocolate. I went back to the Granary on my own.

I had just dropped the board off at the rental shop and was slouching into the reception area when I saw my uncle, sitting on the corner of a sofa wearing jeans and a sweater. I was about

to call out to him – but then I stopped. I knew at once that something was wrong.

It's not easy to explain, but he had never looked like this before. He was completely silent and tense in a way that was almost animal. Ian had dark brown eyes – people say I inherited them – but right now they were cold and colourless. He hadn't noticed me come in. His attention was focused on the reception desk and the man who was checking into the hotel.

People tell a story, Ian had said. *You can read them.* Looking at the man at the reception desk, I tried to do just that.

He was wearing a black roll-neck jersey with dark trousers and a gold Rolex, heavy on his wrist. He had blond hair – an intense yellow and cut short. It almost looked painted on. I would have said he was thirty years old, with a lazy smile. I could hear him talking to the receptionist. He had a Bronx accent.

So much for chapter one. What else could I read in him? His skin was unusually pale. In fact it was almost white, as if he had spent half his life indoors. He worked out; I could see the muscles bulging under his sleeves. And he had very bad teeth. That was strange. Americans wealthy enough to stay in a hotel like this would normally take more care over their dental work.

"You're on the fourth floor, Mr da Silva," the

receptionist said. "Enjoy your stay."

The man had brought a cheap suitcase with him. That was also unusual in the land of Gucci and Louis Vuitton. He picked it up and disappeared into the lift.

I walked further into the reception area and Ian saw me. At once, he relaxed. But he knew I had been watching him.

"Is everything OK?" I asked.

"Yes."

"Who was that?"

"The man who just checked in? I don't know." Ian shook his head as if trying to dismiss the whole thing. "I thought I knew him from somewhere. How was Bear Creek?"

He obviously didn't want to talk about it, so I went up to my room, showered and changed for dinner. As I made my way back downstairs, I noticed one of the secret service men coming out of their room. He walked off down the corridor without saying anything to me. Sahara and her father weren't around.

We ate. We talked. Ian ordered half a bottle of wine for himself and a Coke for me. I must have been more tired than I thought, because at around half past ten I found myself yawning. Ian suggested I go up and watch TV.

"What about you?" I asked.

"Oh ... I might get a breath of air. I'll follow you up later."

I left him and went back to the room, and that was when I discovered I didn't have the electronic card that would open the door. I must have left it inside when I was getting changed. I went back to the dining room. Ian was no longer there. Remembering what he had said, I followed him outside.

And there he was. I will never forget what I saw that night.

There was a courtyard round the side of the hotel, covered with snow, a frozen fountain in the middle. It was surrounded by walls on three sides, with the hotel roofs – also snow-covered – slanting steeply down. The whole area was lit by a full moon, which shone down like a prison searchlight.

Ian Rider and the man who called himself da Silva were locked together, standing like some bizarre statue in the middle of the courtyard. They were fighting for control of a single gun, which was clasped in their hands, high above their heads. I could see the strain on both their faces. But what made the scene even more surreal was that neither of them was making any sound. In fact they were barely moving. Both were focused on the gun. Whichever brought it down would be able to use it on the other.

I called out. It was a stupid thing to do. I could have got my uncle killed. But both men turned to look at me, and it was Ian who took advantage of the interruption. He let go of the gun and slammed his elbow into da Silva's stomach, then bent his arm up, the side of his hand scything the other man's wrist. I had already been learning karate for seven years and recognized the perfectly executed sideways block.

The gun flew out of the man's hand, slid across the snow and came to rest just in front of the fountain.

"Go back, Alex!" my uncle shouted.

It took him less than two seconds but it was enough to lose him the advantage. Da Silva lashed out, the heel of his hand pounding into Ian's chest, winding him. A moment later, the blond man wheeled round in a vicious roundhouse kick. My uncle tried to avoid it, but the snow, the slippery surface, didn't help. He was thrown off his feet and went crashing down. Da Silva stopped and caught his breath. His mouth was twisted in an ugly sneer, his teeth grey in the moonlight. He knew the fight was over. He had won.

That was when I acted. I dived forward, throwing myself onto my stomach and sliding across the ice. My own momentum carried me as far as the gun. I snatched it up, noticing for the first time that it was fitted with a silencer. I had never held a handgun before. It was much heavier than I had expected. Da Silva stared at me.

"No!" My uncle uttered the single word quietly. It didn't matter what the circumstances were. He didn't want me to kill a man.

I couldn't do that. I knew it, even as I lifted the gun and pulled the trigger. I emptied the chamber – all seven bullets – but not at da Silva. I shot into the air above him, over his head. I felt the gun jerking in my hand. The recoil hurt my wrist. But then it was over. The gun was empty. All the bullets had been fired.

Da Silva reached behind him and took out a second gun. My uncle was still on the ground; there was nothing he could do. I lay where I was, my breath coming out in white clouds. Da Silva raised his gun. I could see him deciding which one of us he was going to kill first.

And then there was a gentle rumble and a ton of snow slid off the roof directly above him. I had cut a dotted line with the bullets and – as I had hoped – the weight of the snow had done the rest. Da Silva just had time to look up before the avalanche hit him. I think he opened his mouth – either to swear or to scream – but it was too late. The snow made almost no sound, just a soft *thwump* as it hit. In a second, he had gone. Buried under a huge white curtain.

My uncle got to his feet. I did the same. The two of us looked at each other.

"Do you think we should dig him up?" I asked.

He shook his head. "No. Let's leave him to chill out."

"Who was he? Why did he have a gun? Why were you fighting him?"

There were so many things I wanted to know when we finally got back to our room. Ian had phoned the police. They were already on the way, he told me. He would talk to them when they arrived. The gun that he had taken from da Silva was beside him. I could still feel the weight of it in my hand. My wrist was aching from the recoil; I had never fired a handgun before.

"Forget about it, Alex," he said. "I recognized da Silva from a news story. He's a wanted criminal. Bank fraud..."

"Bank fraud?" I could hardly believe it.

"I met him outside quite by chance. I challenged him – which was pretty stupid of me. He pulled out the gun ... and the rest you saw." Ian smiled. "I expect he'll have frozen solid by now. At least he won't be needing a morgue."

If I'd thought a little more, I'd have realized that none of it added up. When I had come upon the two men, they had been fighting for control of a single gun. They had dropped it – and then da Silva had produced a second gun of his own. So logic should have told me that the first gun belonged to my uncle. But why would he have brought a gun with him on a skiing holiday? How could he even have got it through airport security? It was such an unlikely thought – Ian carrying a firearm – that it had never occurred to me, and I accepted his story because there was no alternative.

Anyway, I was exhausted. It had been a long day and I was glad to crawl into bed. The next morning, Ian told me he wouldn't be coming skiing. Apparently he'd spoken to the police when they finally arrived, and they wanted him to go to the precinct and tell them as much as he could about da Silva and the fight outside the hotel. The bad news was, da Silva had got away.

"He must have burrowed out," Ian said over breakfast – boiled eggs and grilled bacon. He never ate anything fried.

"Do you think he'll come back?" I asked. The thought made me a little nervous.

Ian shook his head. "I doubt it. He knows I recognized him and he's probably out of Colorado by now. Maybe he's even left the States. He won't want to hang around."

"How long do you think you'll be?"

"A few hours. Don't let this spoil the holiday, Alex. Just put it out of your mind. You can ski with Sahara today. She'll be glad to have you on your own."

But Sahara wasn't in her room. When

I knocked on her door, it was opened by her father, Cameron Sands.

"I'm sorry, Alex," he said. "You're too late. She left a few minutes ago; she's got a lesson this morning. But she'll probably call in later – I can ask her to meet you."

"Thanks," I said. "I'll be up at Bear Creek."

He nodded and closed the door, and as he did so I looked over his shoulder and saw that he wasn't alone. The two young men were with him: one sitting on the sofa, the other standing by the window. The secret service men. I could see his desk too. There, as always, was the laptop, surrounded by a pile of papers. If this was a holiday, I wondered what Cameron Sands did when he was at work.

I went downstairs to the boot room and a few minutes later was clumping out to the ski lift with my skis over my shoulder and my poles dragging behind me. I wondered if Sahara would be able to find me if she came looking. There were quite a few people around, and the thing about skiers is that they all look more or less the same. On the other hand, I was wearing a bright green jacket – a North Face Free Thinker. She'd already joked about the colour and I was sure she'd recognize it a mile away.

But as it turned out, I saw her before she saw me. The nearest lift to the hotel was a gondola, taking twenty people at a time up to an area called Black Ridge, about a thousand metres higher up. Sahara was right at the front of the queue, standing between two men. I knew right away they weren't ski instructors. They were too close to her, sandwiching her between them as if they didn't want to let her slip away. One of them was round-faced, fat and white. The other looked Korean or Japanese. Neither of them was smiling. They were both big men – even with the ski suits I got a sense of overworked muscle. Sahara was scared, I saw that too. And a moment later, I saw why.

A third man had gone ahead of them and was waiting inside the gondola. I only glimpsed his face behind the glass but I recognized it instantly. It was da Silva. His hood was up and he was wearing sunglasses, but his pale skin and ugly teeth were unmistakable. He was waiting while the other men joined him with the girl.

I started towards them, but I was already too late. Sahara was inside the gondola. The doors slid shut and the whole thing jerked forward, rising up over the snow. Sahara caught sight of me just as she was swept away. Her eyes widened and she jerked her head in the direction of the hotel. The message was obvious. *Get help!*

I didn't need telling twice. Sahara was being

kidnapped in broad daylight. It was crazy but there could be no doubt about it.

I turned round and began to run...

If it had been six months later, I might have tried to do something myself. The men weren't expecting trouble. I might have gone after them, taking the next gondola and tracking them down. It might have occurred to me to stop the gondola in mid-air. But, of course, everything was very different right then. I was thirteen years old. I was on my own in an American ski resort. And I wasn't even certain about what I'd just seen. Could I really be sure that Sahara was being kidnapped? And if so, why? According to my uncle, da Silva had been involved in some sort of bank fraud. Why would he be interested in the daughter of...

But Cameron Sands worked for the government. He travelled with his own entourage of secret service men. That was when I knew I was right. Whatever was happening to his daughter, it must be aimed at him. He was the one I had to tell.

I stabbed my skis and poles into a mound of snow and ran back as fast as I could to the hotel – not easy in ski boots. I was sweating by the time I got there. You were meant to take your boots off in a room downstairs, but I just clomped right in, through the recep-

tion area, into the lift and up to the second floor. Because of the layout of the hotel, I got to my room before Sahara's, and, acting on impulse, I went in. Ian had said he was heading off to the police precinct, but there was always a chance he would still be there. If I told him what had happened, he would know what to do.

But he had already gone. I turned round and was about to go next door when I heard someone talking. I recognized the voice. It was Sahara's dad. He was standing outside on the terrace, talking into a phone.

I went over to the French window and saw him at once. He was holding the hotel phone – they were all cordless – and standing with his back to me. I could tell straight away that there was something very wrong. He was completely still and his whole body was rigid, like he'd just been electrocuted. I heard him speak.

"Where is she? What have you done with her?"

Da Silva. It had to be him at the end of the phone, calling on a mobile. He'd taken the girl and now he was talking to the dad, just like in the movies. What was he demanding? Money? Somehow, I didn't think so. The Granary wasn't the most expensive hotel at the resort by a long way, and if you were into the money-with-menaces business, there were plenty of film stars and multimillionaires to choose from.

Gently, I slid the window open so I could hear more.

"OK." Sands spoke slowly. In the cold air his breath was white smoke, curling around him. "I'll bring it. And I'll come alone. But I'm warning you..."

Whoever he was talking to had already cut him off. Sands lowered his arm, the phone loose in his hand.

And as far as I was concerned, that should have been it. I liked Sahara, but I hardly knew her. Her dad had two secret service men somewhere in the hotel. Maybe they were still in the room, waiting for him to come back inside. This was none of my business.

But somehow I couldn't leave it there. At the very least, I had to know what was going to happen. It was like getting to a good bit in a book and having to turn the page. I told myself that I wasn't going to get involved, that I was being stupid. But I still couldn't hold back. When Cameron Sands came out of his room five minutes later, I was waiting for him in the corridor.

I followed him downstairs. He had changed into his ski suit with his goggles around his neck and – here was the weird thing – he was carrying the laptop I had seen on the desk. It

was sticking out of a black nylon bag. As he went downstairs he pushed it inside and fastened the zip. There was no sign of the secret service men – but I'd heard what he had said on the phone: he wasn't going to involve them. Wherever he was heading, he was going there alone.

I waited outside the boot room, then followed Sands across the front of the hotel to the gondola, picking up my skis and poles on the way. He had his skis too. The laptop was hanging around his chest in its nylon bag, slightly hidden under one arm. There weren't many people at the gondola now. Ski school had begun and the various classes were already practising their snowploughs on the lower slopes. I watched Sahara's dad hold his lift pass out to be scanned, waited a few moments and then did the same. By now I'd pulled up my hood and put on my own goggles. We got into the same gondola and stood only a few inches apart. But even if he looked in my direction, I knew he wouldn't recognize me. Anyway, he wasn't taking any notice of the people around him. He looked sick with worry. His eyes were fixed on the mountain peaks high above.

Five minutes later we got out at Black Ridge, a sort of wide shelf in the mountains, with another three lifts climbing towards it from different directions. He put on his skis and I did the same. I knew that Cameron Sands was a strong skier, but I reckoned I could keep up with him.

I didn't need to worry. He only skied as far as the nearest lift – a double chair – and took it up to Gun Hill. There was just one more lift that went up from here. It led to an area called the Needle. It was as high as you could get, so high that even on a bright day like today the clouds licked the surface of the snow. Once again I went with him, just a few chairs behind.

Da Silva was waiting for him at the Needle.

After we got off the lift I stayed behind, watching as Cameron Sands skied down about thirty metres to a flat area beside the piste known as Breakneck Pass. The name tells you all you need to know. It was the only way down, a double black diamond run of ice and moguls that started with a stomach-churning, zigzagging chute, continued along the edge of a precipice and then plunged into a wood, with no obvious way between the trees. Not many people came up here. My uncle said you'd need nerves of steel to take on Breakneck. Or a death wish.

And there they all were, waiting with da Silva: the Korean and the fat man I had seen at the gondola and, still trapped between them, a scared-looking Sahara. Nobody could see me. I was thirty metres higher up, and the clouds and snow flurries chasing along the mountain ridge separated me from them. I wiped the ice off my goggles and watched as the scene played out. Cameron Sands said something. Sahara started forward, but the two men held her back. Now it was da Silva's turn. He was smiling. I saw him point at the laptop. Sands hesitated, but not for long. He lifted it off his shoulder and held it in front of him as if weighing it, then handed it over. Da Silva nodded to his companions. They let Sahara go and she slithered – I wouldn't even call it skiing – across to her dad. He put an arm around her. The business was finished.

Except that it wasn't. I hadn't decided what I was going to do until I did it. Suddenly I found myself racing down the slope, my legs bent and my shoulders low, my poles tucked under my arms, picking up as much speed as I could. Nobody was looking my way. They didn't realize I was there until it was too late. But the next moment I was right in the centre of them, moving so fast that I must have been no more than a blur. Da Silva was still holding the laptop. I snatched it out of his hands and kept going, over the lip and down the first stretch of Breakneck Pass.

The next few seconds were a nightmare as

I found myself almost falling off the edge of the mountain, poling like crazy to avoid the first moguls and, at the same time, managing to get the strap over my head so that the computer was out of the way, dangling behind my back. I nearly fell twice. If I'd had time to think what I was doing, I'd probably have lost control and broken both my legs. But instinct had taken over. I was twenty metres down the chute and heading for the next segment before da Silva even knew what had happened.

He didn't hang around. I heard a shout and somehow I knew, without looking back, that the three men were after me. Well, that was sort of what I'd expected. Da Silva wanted the computer. Sands had given it to him. So he and his daughter were no longer needed. I was the target now. All I had to do was get down to the bottom, which couldn't be more than two or three thousand metres from here. It was just a pity there was no one else around. If I could get back into a crowd, I'd be safe.

I heard a crack. A bullet slammed into the snow, inches from my left ski. Who had fired? The answer was obvious, but even so I found it hard to believe. Was it really possible to ski in these conditions and bring out a gun at the same time? The snow was horrible, wind-packed and hard as metal. My skis were grinding as they carried me over the surface.

I was grateful that my uncle had insisted on choosing my equipment for me: Nordica twin tips, wide under the foot and seriously stiff. It had taken me a while to get used to them, but the whole point was that they were built for speed. Right now they seemed to be flying, and as I carved and pivoted around the moguls I almost wanted to laugh. I didn't think anyone in the world would be able to catch up with me.

I was wrong. Either da Silva and his men had spent a long time training for this, or they'd been experts to begin with. I came to a gully and risked a glance back. There were less than fifteen metres between us and the men were gaining fast. Worse still, they didn't even seem to be exerting themselves. They had that slow, fluid quality you get in only the best skiers. They could have been cutting their way down a nursery slope. The distance between us was closing all the time. Suddenly I knew that there was nothing to laugh about. I cursed myself for getting involved in the first place. Why had I done it? This had nothing to do with me.

Then I made it to the woodland. At least the trunks and branches would make it harder for anyone to take another shot at me. I was lucky I'd done plenty of tree skiing with Ian. I knew that I had to keep the speed up –

otherwise I'd lose control. But go too fast and I'd risk impaling myself on a branch. The secret is balance. Or luck. Or something.

I didn't really know where I was going. Everything was just streaks of green and brown and white. I was getting tired. Branches were slashing at my face; my legs were already aching with all the twists and turns, and the laptop was half strangling me, threatening to pull me over backwards. One of my skis almost snagged on a root. I shifted my body weight and cried out as my left shoulder slammed into a trunk. It felt like I'd broken a bone. I almost lost control there and then. One of the men shouted something. I couldn't see them but it sounded as if they were right behind me. That gave me new strength. I shot forward onto a miniature ramp, which propelled me up into the air and through a tangle of branches that scratched my face and tore at my goggles.

I was in the clear. The wood disappeared behind me and I fell into a wide, empty area. But I landed badly. My skis slipped away and there was a sickening crash as I dived headlong into the snow. My bones shuddered. Then I was sliding helplessly in a blinding white explosion. My skis came free. I was aware that the surface underneath had changed. It was smoother and more slippery. I was moving faster. I stretched out a hand and tried to stop myself, but there was no purchase at all. Where was I? At last I slowed down and stopped.

I was breathless and confused. I was sure I must have broken several bones. The laptop was round my throat and the ground seemed to be cracking up where I lay. No, it *was* cracking up... As I struggled to my knees, I realized what had happened. I had gone spectacularly off-piste. There was a lake on the west side of the mountain – they called it Coldwater Creek. I had landed right next to it and managed to slide in. I was on the surface of the ice. And it was breaking under my weight.

Da Silva and the two men had stopped on the edge of the lake. All three were facing me. Two of them had guns. My goggles had come off in the fall and da Silva recognized me.

"You!" He spat out the single word. He didn't sound friendly.

There were about ten metres between us. Nobody moved.

"Give me the laptop," he demanded.

I said nothing. If I gave him the laptop, he would kill me. That much I knew.

"Give it to me or I'll take it," he continued.

There was the sound of something cracking. A black line appeared, snaking its way towards my foot. I steadied myself, trying not to breathe. Water, as cold as death, welled up around me. I wondered how much longer the ice would hold. If it broke I would disappear for ever. And if anyone ever did find my body, they wouldn't recognize it.

"Why don't you come and get it," I said.

Da Silva nodded and the Korean man stepped forward. I could see he wasn't too happy about it. I guess he'd been chosen because he was the lightest of the three. But he wasn't light enough. On the third step, the ice broke. One minute he was there, the next he was down, his arms floundering and his face filling with panic as he tried to grip the sides of the hole. He tried to scream but no sound came out. His lungs must already have frozen.

He had taken a gun with him. That only left one other. Da Silva snatched it from the fat man – at least there was no way he was going to trust *his* weight on the ice – and pointed it at me.

"Give me the laptop," he said. "Or I'll shoot you where you stand."

"What will you do then?" I said. I took another step, moving away from the edge of the lake. The ice creaked. I could feel it straining beneath my feet. "You can't reach me. You're too heavy."

"The ice will harden in the night. I'll return for it tomorrow."

"You think it'll still be working? A whole day and a night out here?"

"Give it to me!" Da Silva didn't want to argue any more. I could see his finger tightening on the trigger. I had absolutely no doubt that he was about to kill me.

"Alex … get down. Now!"

My uncle's voice came from the wood. As da Silva spun round, I dropped low, hoping the sudden movement wouldn't crack the ice. At the same time there were two shots. Da Silva had fired first. He'd missed. My uncle hadn't. Da Silva seemed to throw his own gun away. He had been hit in the shoulder. He sank to his knees, gripping the wound. Blood, bright red in the morning sun, seeped through his fingers.

Ian Rider appeared. I had no idea how he'd managed to follow us down from the Needle. I'd never so much as glimpsed him. But that must have been what he'd done. He skied to the very edge of the lake and spoke to me, his eyes never leaving da Silva or the other man.

"Are you all right, Alex?" he asked.

"Yes."

"Come back over here. Give me the laptop. Get your skis back on."

I did as he told me. I'd begun to tremble. I'd like to say it was just the cold, but I'm not sure that would be true.

"Who are you?" da Silva demanded. I'd

never heard a voice so full of hate.

"Your skis. Both of you..." My uncle raised the gun. The two men took off their skis. He gestured. They knew what to do. Da Silva and the fat man threw their skis into the lake. Meanwhile, the Korean had managed to pull himself out. He was lying there shivering, blue with cold.

I snapped my skis back on.

"Enjoy the rest of the day, gentlemen," my uncle said, and we set off together. Da Silva and the others would have to walk down. It would take them hours – and I had no doubt that the police would be waiting for them when they arrived.

And that was it really. What you might call my first mission.

Sahara and her dad left that day. I thought I'd never see them again, but in fact I met Sahara a couple of years later, and it was from her I learnt that her dad had been working in the office of the Secretary of Defense. His hard drive had contained classified information about the withdrawal of American troops from Iraq. If it had leaked, the result would have been a huge embarrassment for the US government. Someone must have paid da Silva to steal it, but when that failed he had engineered the kidnap and the attempted ransom. Something like that anyway.

I never did find out how my uncle arrived just in time to rescue me. He said it was just luck, that he'd seen da Silva on the gondola and followed him up the mountain while I was racing back to the hotel. Maybe that was true. He also said the gun he'd used was the same gun he'd snatched in the fight the night before. That certainly wasn't. The funny thing was, we hardly talked about it again while we were in Colorado. It was as if there was an unspoken agreement between us. Ask me no questions and I'll tell you no lies.

When I look back on it, I wonder how stupid I could have been not to see what Ian Rider really was. But then again, I didn't know what I was either – what he'd made me. I remember he pretended to be very angry that I'd put myself in danger. But at the same time I could see he was secretly pleased. He'd been training me all my life to follow in his footsteps, and what happened at Gunpoint showed him I was ready.

And that was just as well. In a few months' time, I'd need to be.